Uncle Sam's Family

P9-DMY-722
ONED

SUNY Series in Interdisciplinary Perspectives in Social History
Harvey J. Graff, Editor

Robert V. Wells

UNCLE SAM'S FAMILY

Issues in and Perspectives on American Demographic History

State University of New York Press
ALBANY

Published by
State University of New York Press, Albany

©1985 State University of New York

All rights reserved

Printed in the United States of America

No part of this book may be used or reproduced
in any manner whatsoever without written permission
except in the case of brief quotations embodied in critical articles and reviews.

For information, address State University of New York
Press, State University Plaza, Albany, N.Y., 12246

Library of Congress Cataloging in Publication Date

ISBN 0-87395-962-0
ISBN 0-87395-963-9 (pbk.)

10 9 8 7 6 5 4 3 2 1

Wells, Robert V., 1943-
Uncle Sam's family.

(SUNY series in interdisciplinary perspectives in social history)
Bibliography: p. 168
1. United States—Population—History. I. Title.
II. Series.
HB3505.W42 1985 304.6'0973 84-8733
ISBN 0-87395-962-0
ISBN 0-87395-963-9 (pbk.)

Contents

Illustrations

Tables

Preface

In the spring of 1980, Harvey Graff offered me the opportunity to contribute a volume on current issues in American demographic history to the State University of New York Press Series in Interdisciplinary Perspectives in Social History, which was to aid in, "the introduction of the results and conceptualization of the so-called 'new social history' into the classroom." I accepted the offer and what follows is the result.

My goals in writing this book have been first, to introduce readers to the origins of interest in particular aspects of demographic history; second, to indicate the sources and techniques by which answers to demographic questions can be obtained; third, to discuss the current answers to some of the most interesting and important questions in terms of both detailed findings and theoretical significance; and fourth, to suggest how the results improve our understanding of American history.

Because American demographic history is a very large and complex subject, a number of choices had to be made. From the start, I intended the work for use in the classroom by students largely unfamiliar with the material. Although I would be pleased if specialists in the field find the book helpful, I do not expect they will be greatly surprised by what I have to say. In addition, limits of space required selecting only some of the many possible topics. Obviously, another author might well have written about a somewhat different set of subjects. This is especially true when the focus shifts from a discussion of what we already know to areas where important research may appear in the future. If something has been omitted, that does not necessarily imply the topic is unimportant, only that I wanted to write about other matters.

In twenty years of research and writing on demographic history I have acquired numerous debts to other scholars in the field. They deserve a collective thanks. I also wish to thank the publishers who have agreed to let me use various maps, tables, and graphs in the text. Full recognition will be given at each appropriate place. Ellen Fladger, Archivist at Schaffer Library, Union College, and Jean V. Kristiansson,

Executive Secretry of the New England Society in the City of New York, have provided special assistance. Finally, as every author knows, it is one's family who deserve the greatest thanks, sometimes for direct help, but always for putting up with the personal quirks of an author at work. Thank you Cathie, Lisa, and Vanessa.

Chapter 1

Introduction: Understanding our World

A Look at the Past

A hundred years ago, Mark Twain wrote a story about a Connecticut Yankee factory worker who received a blow on the head and awoke to find himself in King Arthur's England. One of Twain's purposes in writing this story was to contrast the newly emerging technological and economic arrangements of late nineteenth-century America to those of the medieval world. He also commented extensively on the values each society felt were important to sustain its way of life. What Twain either did not see or did not think worthy of note were equally remarkable contrasts in such fundamental aspects of life as patterns of birth, death, marriage, and migration. In addition, he by and large ignored any differences in family arrangements between the nineteenth century and earlier times.

Imagine, therefore, that the same thing happens to you. Walking down a crowded city street, you are jostled and lose your balance, fall, and strike your head on a curb. When you wake up, you find yourself in a completely unfamiliar environment. As your head begins to clear, you realize that you are on the edge of a very small village. Later, you discover that this village is located in New Jersey, and the time is 1750.

As you sit by the roadside, you notice a group of people coming toward you. As they pass, you realize that this is a funeral procession. This is not too surprising, because in the middle of the eighteenth century death was a very common part of life. Because of where you are sitting, the people in the procession do not see you, so you are able to observe them rather closely as they go by. One of the things that strikes your attention is that the coffin is remarkably small. It is clearly that of a child. This, also, you learn later is not unusual, because children commonly died during this time period. The second thing that surprises you is that the individuals following the coffin to the graveyard seem to accept their loss relatively calmly. You will later learn that since so many children die at a relatively early age, parents do not invest significant amounts of emotional energy in their children until they have survived the first five or ten years of life. In addition, their religious beliefs encourage many colonists to view death not as an ending, but as a release from earthly miseries and sins.

As you watch the procession go by, you realize that about half the people in the procession are children, including several you later learn are brothers and sisters of the deceased. There seem to be no extremely old people in this solemn group of New Jerseyites and, indeed, you discover later, that all the grandparents had died several years before. Although it seems natural to you, it is somewhat surprising that both parents are present, for this was not always the case in the eighteenth century when death was extraordinarily common.

Since you are on the edges of the village and the whole area has a rather unsettled look, you are not quite sure where to go. Therefore, you decide to wait for the procession to return from the graveyard. As family and friends straggle back toward the village, you step out and stop an older man who seems to be in charge of this gathering and ask him for help. The man, who is in fact the head of the family, and a prominent citizen in the community, is quite startled by your unexpected appearance and responds with a good deal of suspicion. To begin, he thinks your clothes are extremely odd and your accent rather unusual. You later learn that migrants were not always welcomed in American communities during the eighteenth century, even though they may be relatively familiar. And if, by chance, you are female or black the suspicion would be even greater, with the man wondering why you are wandering alone, without the supervision or permission of an adult, white male. If you had happened to be Hispanic or Asian, the man would have been even more startled, because you would be a type of person entirely unfamiliar to this American colonist.

You ask to join him and return to his community. After a few minutes of thought, he reluctantly agrees, and reassures you that you need have no fear with regard to the death of his child. The child, he reports, had not died from anything so severe as the pox, but rather had succumbed to the bloody flux, both terms with which you are unfamiliar. Nevertheless, he is concerned with your possible safety and asks if you have been seasoned. You express some uncertainty about what that means. He asks whether you have been in the colonies long enough to have become accustomed to the diseases that are common there. You tell him that you have just arrived, sparing him the details of your trip, and reassure him that although you have not been seasoned you do have all your immunizations, a reference that he clearly does not understand.

As you arrive in town with this small, sombre procession, you are struck immediately by two things. First, the town you are entering is, in reality, a small cluster of houses containing no more than a couple of hundred inhabitants. The village is full of children and animals roaming loose, with a variety of strange sights, smells, and sounds that are dramatically different from those of the city in which you have been living.

After conferring with the other men who lead this community, many of whom are related to your acquaintance, he reports that it is possible for you to remain in this village, at least for a few weeks. However, he informs you that you will have to stay with his family because the community considers single persons to be dangerous if they live alone, and, in addition, housing is relatively scarce and it is a waste of resources to let any one individual have a complete dwelling for his or her own personal use. He also informs you that you must agree to put yourself under his authority because there are no police in the village and the chief citizens feel it necessary to keep you well supervised while you are there.

After several weeks in this town, you have decided that life in eighteenth-century America is extraordinarily dull. The food, though ample and relatively well balanced, is generally plain and does not have a great deal of variety at any particular time of year. In addition, because there are no refrigerators available, it is often somewhat spoiled. The house in which you live seems rather crowded, both because it is not terribly large and because there are five children still living at home, as well as the two parents. You discover that there is no privacy for yourself, or for anyone else for that matter. However, this seems to bother only you, for the others have obviously grown up without a chance to retire to one's own room.

You quickly learn that the family expects you to join them in their work around the house and in the fields they are cultivating. However, the heavy labor expected of you involved weeding and harvesting during the summer, cleaning the barns and taking care of the cattle, and working in the garden, things to which you are not used. The work you do depends whether you are male or female. Often you will work exclusively with members of your own sex, with men in the fields and women in the house and garden. However, tasks such as the care of animals, harvesting crops, slaughtering hogs, or the production of soap required joint efforts. Likewise, bad weather, which required men and women to work inside, turned the house into a common workshop, even though the various members of the family were doing different things.

There is almost nothing by way of excitement in this community other than to go to church on Sunday morning. It is clear that both the family and the community expect you to conform to their patterns; they have no interest in your own individual needs or expectations. A chance remark to one of the children in the family, who is approximately your age, that you are a college student seems to give you a significant increase in status within both the family and the community, since such levels of education are rare indeed. If, by chance, you are female or black, the community might well express considerable wonder, and possible disapproval, at educational resources being squandered on such a presumably inferior person. A comment that you are going to college in order to find yourself brings a look of incomprehension from your hosts. After you explain what you mean by this remark, they ask how you will fulfill the needs of your family and your community if you continue to seek to find yourself. Your response to this is uncertain, partly because you are no longer sure where the line between family and community falls in the town in which you are living.

After several weeks in this small town, word comes that an epidemic of smallpox has broken out in a neighboring village. At this point, you decide to move on, for although you have been vaccinated against smallpox you do not wish to see this ugly killer. Several of your new friends and acquaintances bear the pockmarks from earlier exposure to this disease, and their descriptions of what a smallpox epidemic can be like makes it clear to you that you do not wish to be present if the disease manages to transfer itself from one community to the other.

Deciding that life in a similar village or in even more rural areas is not for you, you ask your way to the nearest big city. You are startled to find that New York City is the nearest one, although it has, at this time, somewhat less than 20,000 people. In fact, you learn that only Boston, Massachusetts, Newport, Rhode Island, Philadelphia, Pennsylvania, and Charleston, South Carolina, are worthy of the name "town" in all the colonies on the North Atlantic seaboard from Massachusetts to South Carolina, and these are all ports.

Because there are only a million people living in the colonies from New Hampshire to Georgia, and northern New Jersey is still very much a frontier in the middle of the eighteenth century, travel is frequently difficult in these thinly settled territories. Therefore, you decide to head to New York City rather than one of the more distant towns. Before you can get to New York, however, your horse veers, and, being an inexperienced rider, you fall off and strike your head on a rock in the road. Waking up, you discover you have returned to the late twentieth century.

Curious about your experience, you want to find out about how typical the town and family in which you lived were and how common were the values held by your newfound friends. In addition, you want to know when and how the changes began that make life in the twentieth century so different. A few hours research in your local library leads to several important discoveries. A number of people have been studying these same questions, though without the deep personal interest that you have, and you find it is important to look at three different things to help you understand the questions you have raised. First, it is important to gain some idea about the theories of demographic history, for you discover that it is very much involved in your interests. Second, the sources of information about the demographic patterns of individuals and groups in the past also must be examined with some care. Finally, you become aware that you will need a surprising variety of skills in order to assemble the data you need to make meaningful comparisons into appropriate forms, and to interpret the patterns that emerge from that evidence.

Theories and Themes

The central demographic theory that tries to describe and explain how life in the eighteenth century has evolved into the present is known as the "theory of demographic transition." In its simplest form, transition theory describes the change from the past to the present as follows. In earlier centuries, population growth was remarkably slow, with both births and deaths occurring quite frequently. The most significant year-to-year variation a population experienced was in the number of deaths. When epidemics struck a community, the death rate could soar, but in years when there was no unusual mortality and the harvests were good, there were relatively few deaths. Childbearing, however, is assumed to have remained at a relatively high, constant level throughout. Eventually the death rate began to fall, perhaps because of improvements in medical care, but more likely because of better standards of living resulting from a more ample and better balanced diet, improved housing, better clothing, and similar changes. Countries that have experienced this decline in the death rate are assumed to have had a period of relatively high population growth because the birth rate temporarily remained high. This period of rapid growth began, depending on the nation under study, sometime from the mid-eighteenth to the late-nineteenth centuries. In recent years, countries where this change has occurred have once again returned to relatively low rates of population growth, because the birth rate eventually began to fall along with the death rate and both have become balanced at relatively low levels. However, after the period of transition is over, the assumption is that any variation in short-term growth rates will be the result of fluctuations in the birth rate rather than the death rate.

The demographic transition theory is extremely interesting to those who are concerned with whether countries with either rapid population growth today or the potential for rapid growth can repeat the experience of those countries that have gone through the demographic transition. Most of the countries that have substantially completed the change are either European or are on the eastern fringes of Asia. Early observers of the demographic transition frequently pointed out that the basic demographic changes often occurred in conjuction with considerable economic growth, widespread industrialization, the movement of a large proportion of the people into urban areas, and a high level of literacy.

Some scholars concluded that economic change produced the demographic change, and so any problems from population growth in countries with either rapid growth or the potential for rapid growth could be solved by economic development. They ignored the difficulty of achieving significant economic growth under the conditions where population growth was high. They also ignored the possibility that there might be a close link between well-established demographic patterns and economic arrangements relying on agricultural production. It is possible that both demographic and economic patterns must change together if the transition is to occur. People who are willing to work in new ways may also be willing to experiment with new forms of medical care, new diets, and even with the use of contraception. Conversely, it seems improbable that innovation in one basic aspect of life could occur easily if closely related patterns of behavior maintained their traditional forms.

Recent studies also suggest that the actual historical pattern was more complex than demographic transition theory allows. Pre-transition populations were not as simple and stable as once was thought. They have never been uniform across time or place. Rapid population growth and decline clearly have been part of the human experience well before the nineteenth century. In addition, in some countries, the presumed patterns of cause and effect simply do not fit the actual historical circumstances. In Great Britain, for example, the birth rate seems to have risen, along with a decline in the death rate. In the United States, the birth rate began to decline well before any parallel fall in the death rate, and significantly before any widespread industrialization or urbanization. Furthermore, historians have discovered that birth rates sometimes fell in rural areas, as well as in the urbanizing part of the nation. This does not fit well with classical transition theory.

Thus, much of demographic history is concerned with precisely when, how, and why the changes occured that distinguished 1980 from 1780 in the United States, England, or Japan, and what it is that sets life in the Soviet Union, Germany, or Sweden apart from that in Haiti, Nigeria, or India today. Indeed, the question of what forms of economic, social, and political organization distinguish parts of the world variously described as industrial, developed, or modern from those parts of the world referred to as agricultural, less developed, or traditional is the central concern of almost all social science disciplines and many of the humanities.

In addition to the dominant concern with the demographic transition, there are two other major sources of interest in demographic history. One focuses on what Fernand Braudel refers to in his book, *The Structures of Everyday Life,* as "the limits of the possible." By this Braudel means that in any society certain basic structures of population, technology, and economic production and exchange will define the problems that that society must solve in order to survive. Of course, there may be a variety of solutions, and the choice of a particular solution will depend heavily on the values or culture that society holds. At the same time, not all imaginable solutions are possible in every specific setting. Nevertheless, it is clear patterns of population, in all their manifestations, are important in defining the problems that a particular society must confront and determining what solutions to those problems will or will not work. An understanding of basic demographic patterns can also shed light on why certain clusters of ideas and values were found appealing at various times and others were rejected.

A second source of interest in demographic history that is only loosely connected to the demographic transition is the realization that many of life's most basic changes are connected to one's experiences with birth, death, marriage, and migration. These events frequently mark critical transitions in one's life, whether experienced directly or as part of a family. Births, deaths, marriages, and moving can alter the rhythms of one's life and change roles and responsibilities in family and society. One need think only of the consequences of marrying, of having a first child, or moving to an environment quite different from any previously experienced to realize that these actions often are of greater consequence to individuals than the average election or piece of legislation. Since levels of childbearing, patterns of death, forms of marriage, and the ebbs and flows of migration were dramatically different in the past, the way we look at life today may have little in common with the attitudes and expectations of those who lived under quite different conditons. Thus, it is of considerable interest to gain an understanding of and empathy with an American colonist in 1690 who was struggling to survive under different demographic circumstances. It is perhaps less important to have a detailed understanding of what British officials were doing at the same time that they forced many of the New England colonies into a union known as the Dominion of New England.

Thus, demographic history moves from questions of worldwide consequence spanning several centuries to considerations of the most personal behavior and intimate experiences within local contexts. The fall of Rome to the rise of Poughkeepsie, New York, are both within the realm of demographic history. So, too, are smallpox epidemics, garbage collection, and the use of German in public schools, all issues related to population patterns that disturbed the lives of people living in nineteenth-century Wisconsin. In its own way, your birth is as interesting as the evolution of the Chinese population.

Because American history overlaps the period of demographic transition and the emergence of the modern world so closely, concerns with changes in fertility and mortality, especially since 1800, have attracted wide attention. But there is one other theme that dominates our demographic past and sets our history apart from that of many other nations. That theme is migration.

Although all of Chapter 4 explores some of the varied and complex patterns of migration in American history, at least six major topics relating to migration will be mentioned here because of their importance to any understanding of our nation's history.

One of the most important themes of American history revolving around migration involves questions about the origins of American society. Since the United States emerged from English colonies established on the eastern coast of North America, some have argued that American society was simply a European transplant growing in North America. Others contend that, as early as the seventeenth century, a new environment had brought forth a new American culture or way of life.

Students of migration in American history have frequently

remarked on the wide variety of ethnic, racial, regional, and religious divisions in the United States. Cultural pluralism was initially used to characterize the nineteenth and twentieth centuries, but recently we have discovered that rapid mobility and cultural pluralism were well established in the seventeenth and eighteenth centuries. This discovery marks the second major theme. A third important strand of migration history is very closely bound to the second. It involves the impact of approximately 30 million immigrants on the nature and character of American society between 1820 and 1920. This story is better known than any other aspect of immigration history.

Expansion westward across North America, which helped create a continental nation out of a scattered handful of settlements on the North Atlantic seaboard, marks the fourth theme of interest. This is a complex story of European expansion, Indian contraction, and Afro-Americans traveling first as the involuntary companions of their white masters and, after emancipation, seeking destinations of their own choosing. The topic involves transportation changes, new forms of ownership and distribution of land, the creation of new regions, and the redefinition of old.

Equally important to movement to new agricultural frontiers was migration to a dramatically different frontier, that is, the urban frontier. During the nineteenth century, America was transformed from an agricultural to an urban nation. As part of this process, Americans had to adjust to radically different environments, with new rhythms of work and leisure and new opportunities for and threats to individuals and their families.

Finally, in the twentieth century, migration patterns have altered once again. Widespread restrictions on the numbers and types of immigrants from abroad were imposed for the first time. Black Americans began to leave the southeastern United States for the North and the West, and for urban environments instead of rural areas. Since World War II, movement to what is known as the "Sunbelt" has involved major realignments in where people work, what they do, and their political influence on the federal government. All three of these changes mark major shifts in migration patterns that have had and will continue to have important consequences for American society.

Sources

Demographic history depends heavily on two basic types of sources. Censuses provide the statistical equivalent of a portrait of society at a particular moment. Vital statistics, that is lists of births, deaths, and marriages, offer historians more of a moving picture of how a population grows and changes over time. The vast majority of basic demographic information about the past comes from these two important sources. However, a full understanding of demographic history requires extensive reference to other materials. The chapters that follow discuss a number of specific findings based on the various sources; our interest here is on the sources in general.

A census, in its most basic form, is simply a count of all the people living in a particular region at a particular moment in time. Obviously, this definition raises questions about who is actually living in a particular region, as opposed to just visiting, and how to count people who are temporarily away from their permanent place of residence. However, these matters are generally of relatively small consequence to demographic historians. A census must be distinguished from other lists that provide at least some evidence regarding the size of the population, but do not actually count all the inhabitants of a community. Examples of such lists are rolls of taxpayers, militia, or heads of households. All of these documents record only part of the population. Therefore, if one wishes to estimate the total population, it is necessary to arrive at some conclusion about what proportion taxpayers or soldiers comprise of the total population.

Anyone using censuses quickly discovers that they vary considerably from simple tables, giving the total population of a community, state, or nation, to elaborate lists, in which the name of each person is entered and information about that person is provided describing, among other things, age, sex, race, place of birth, place of previous residence, position in the household if the individual is living in a household, education, and occupation. Tables I and II, taken from the introduction to the published volume of the United States Census of 1850, show how the relatively simple count of 1790 had evolved into a complex study of the American people and their society by 1850. The process has continued through the most recent enumeration in 1980.

Obviously, the more detailed a census the more helpful it is in studying the past; the simplest counts inform us only of total population size, without even indicating how rapidly the population is growing. Even to estimate growth requires at least two separate counts or some detail about the composition of the population. The most complex documents allow remarkably detailed studies of topics of interest to demographic historians such as patterns of childbearing, when and how often people moved from one place to another, patterns of marriage, and the age and sex structure of the total population. If the census covers a wide enough area, then it is possible to explore variations in these structures in different regions within the larger unit.

It is important to keep in mind that there are a number of limits with regard to census data. The cost of taking a census no doubt has some influence on what is included, or omitted, from any survey. Most important, censuses were shaped by the immediate needs and concerns of the people who were doing the counting rather than the needs of the historian who wants to know more about people in the past. Some of the information in a census is based on the direct observation of the responsible officials; other data can be collected only with the cooperation of the people involved. When using information provided by individuals, it is well to keep in mind that people in the eighteenth or nineteenth century probably shared the modern tendency to answer some questions more honestly and accurately than they might others. Planters, for example, might have lied about the number of slaves they owned if they feared taxes levied on their human property. Young men approaching the age of sixteen might have been reluctant to divulge their age accurately if they felt military duty was likely to follow.

Not all errors are necessarily deliberate. Sometimes censuses have sought to retrieve data about the past. For example, older women have been asked about the number of children that they had given birth to throughout their entire marriage. This causes problems, because all human beings have a tendency to forget events that have occurred twenty or thirty years ago, or else they may distort a sequence or pattern of events. Reference to the schedule of the 1850 United States Census shows that enumerators were asked to indicate if a person was insane or idiotic, even though neither of these highly subjective terms was defined. Hence, different enumerators might have recorded the same population differently. An examination of Tables I and II will reveal where distortions might occur in the data that would make some figures more reliable and useful than others.

The censuses that may be used to study American history can be divided into three broad categories. Prior to 1776, when America was under British rule, over forty census were taken in the colonies that made up the original United States. These were produced at irregular intervals, generally as a result of requests for information by British imperial officials to royal governors. The colonists themselves rarely, if ever, saw any particular need to count themselves and their neighbors. Some of these documents were quite detailed, and many of them are actually more informative than the federal censuses taken in the first half century after independence. However, they varied widely in terms of detail, ranging from simple statements of total population to name-by-name lists of inhabitants, in which several characteristics about each individual were noted. In addition, the amount of information available for each colony varies considerably, from the ten quite

Table I. Schedules for Each Census of the United States, 1790–1820

CENSUS OF 1850.

SCHEDULES ADOPTED FOR EACH CENSUS OF THE UNITED STATES FROM 1790.

CENSUS OF 1790.

Names of heads of families.	Free white males of 16 years and upwards, including "heads."	Free white males under 16.	Free white females, including "heads."	All other free.	Slaves.

CENSUS OF 1800.

Name of county, parish, township, town, or city, where the family resides.	Name of head of family.	Free white males under 10.	Free white males of 10 and under 16.	Free white males of 16 and under 26, including "heads."	Free white males of 26 and under 45, including "heads."	Free white males of 45 and upwards, including "heads."	Free white females under 10.	Free white females of 10 and under 16.	Free white females of 16 and under 26, including "heads."	Free white females of 26 and under 45, including "heads."	Free white females of 45 and upwards, including "heads."	All other free, except Indians not taxed.	Slaves.

CENSUS OF 1810.

Name of county, parish, township, town, or city, &c.	Name of head of family.	Free white males under 10 years of age.	Free white males of 10 and under 16.	Free white males of 16 and under 26, including "heads."	Free white males of 26 and under 45, including "heads."	Free white males of 45 and upwards, including "heads."	Free white females under 10 years of age.	Free white females of 10 and under 16.	Free white females of 16 and under 26, including "heads."	Free white females of 26 and under 45, including "heads."	Free white females of 45 and upwards, including "heads."	All other free persons, except Indians not taxed.	Slaves.

CENSUS OF 1810—MANUFACTURES.

Cotton manufacturing establishments.	Cotton duck.	Hempen manufacturing establishments.	Blended and unnamed cloths and stuffs.	Tow cloth.	Woolen manufacturing establishments.	Cotton and wool spun in mills.	Web, lace, and fringe.	Stockings.	Looms for cloths of cotton, wool, &c.	Carding machines.	Fulling mills.	Sewing silk and raw silk.	Jennies.	Spindles.	Wire card manufactories.	Spinning wheels.	Hatteries.	Furnaces.	Bar iron, &c.	Trip hammers.	Rolling and slitting mills.	Naileries.	Wire drawing.	Gunsmiths.	Blacksmiths' work.	Steel furnaces.	Hydraulic engine makers.	Tacks.	Clocks and watches.	Gold and silver work.	Tin plate work.	Manufactures of mixed metals.	Copper and brass manufactures.	Bells.	Buttons.	Lead.	Tallow candles.	Soap.	Spermaceti candles.	Spermaceti oil.	Whale oil.	Spermaceti and whale oil.	Tanneries.	Boots, shoes, and slippers.	Saddlery.	Morocco skins.	Leather gloves.	Cat-gut.	Flax seed oil.	Spirits distilled from grain.	Spirits distilled from molasses.	All kinds of spirits distilled.	Beer.	Shipping.	Cabinet work.	Chairs.	Carriage makers.	Wagons.	Wooden ware unnamed.	Rakes.	Essence of spruce.	Oil or essence of turpentine.	Sugar refined.	Paper.	Playing cards.	Marble saw-mills.	&c., &c., &c., &c.

Many other similar heads were added, and the statistics taken of the number of establishments, amount produced, value, &c.

CENSUS OF 1820.

	Name of the county, parish, township, town, or city.
	Names of heads of families.
WHITES.	Free white males under 10.
	Free white males of 10 and under 16.
	Free white males between 16 and 18.
	Free white males of 16 and under 26, including "heads."
	Free white males of 26 and under 45, including "heads."
	Free white males of 45 and upwards, including "heads."
	Free white females under 10 years of age.
	Free white females of 10 and under 16.
	Free white females of 16 and under 26, including "heads."
	Free white females of 26 and under 45, including "heads" of families.
	Free white females of 45 and upwards, including "heads."
	Foreigners not naturalized.
SLAVES.	Males under 14.
	Males of 14 and under 26.
	Males of 26 and under 45.
	Males of 45 and upwards.
	Females of 14.
	Females of 14 and under 26.
	Females of 26 and under 45.
	Females of 45 and upwards.
FREE COLORED.	Males under 14 years.
	Males of 14 and under 26.
	Males of 26 and under 45.
	Males of 45 and upwards.
	Females under 14 years.
	Females of 14 and under 26.
	Females of 26 and under 45.
	Females of 45 and upwards.
	All other persons, except Indians not taxed.
	Foreigners not naturalized.
	Number of persons engaged in agriculture.
	Number of persons engaged in commerce.
	Number of persons engaged in manufactures.

CENSUS OF 1820—MANUFACTURES.

PLACE.	Name of the county, parish, township, town, or city.
RAW MATERIALS EMPLOYED.	The kind.
	Quantity annually consumed.
	Cost of annual consumption.
NUMBER OF PERSONS EMPLOYED.	Men.
	Women.
	Boys and girls.
MACHINERY.	Quantity and kind of machinery.
	Quantity of machinery in operation.
EXPENDITURES.	Capital invested.
	Paid annually for wages.
	The contingent expenses.
PRODUCTION.	Nature and names of articles manufactured.
VALUE OF PRODUCTION.	Market value of articles annually manufactured.
GENERAL REMARKS.	Past and present condition of the establishment; the demand for, and sale of, its manufactures.

SOURCE: U.S. Bureau of the Census, *The Seventh Census of the United States: 1850* (Robert Armstrong, printer, Washington, D.C., 1853), x.

Table II. Schedule of the United States Census of 1850

CENSUS OF 1850.

CENSUS OF 1850.

SCHEDULE No. 1.—FREE INHABITANTS.

Dwelling-houses numbered in the order of visitation.	Families numbered in the order of visitation.	Name of every person whose usual place of abode on the 1st day of June, 1850, was in this family.	DESCRIPTION.			Profession, occupation, or trade of each male person over 15 years of age.	Value of real estate owned.	Place of birth, naming the State, Territory, or country.	Married within the year.	Attended school within the year.	Persons over 20 years of age who cannot read and write.	Whether deaf and dumb, blind, insane, idiotic, pauper, or convict.
			Age.	Sex.	Color—white, black, or mulatto.							

SCHEDULE No. 2.—SLAVES.

Name of slave owners.	Number of slaves.	DESCRIPTION.			Fugitives from the State.	Number manumitted.	Deaf and dumb, blind, insane, or idiotic.	Remarks.
		Age.	Sex.	Color.				

SCHEDULE No. 4.—PRODUCTIONS OF AGRICULTURE.

Name of owner, agent, or manager of the farm.	Acres of land improved.	Acres of land unimproved.	Cash value of farm.	Value of farming implements and machinery.	LIVE STOCK, JUNE 1, 1850.								PRODUCE DURING THE YEAR ENDING JUNE 1, 1850.																																
					Horses.	Mules and asses.	Working oxen.	Milch cows.	Other cattle.	Sheep.	Swine.	Value of live stock.	Value of animals slaughtered during the year.	Wheat, bushels of.	Rye, bushels of.	Indian corn, bushels of.	Oats, bushels of.	Rice, pounds of.	Tobacco, pounds of.	Ginned cotton, bales of 400 lbs. each.	Wool, pounds of.	Beans and peas, bushels of.	Buckwheat, bushels of.	Barley, bushels of.	Irish potatoes, bushels of.	Sweet potatoes, bushels of.	Value of orchard products in dollars.	Wine, gallons of.	Value of produce of market gardens.	Butter, pounds of.	Cheese, pounds of.	Hay, tons of.	Clover seed, bushels of.	Other grass seeds, bushels of.	Hops, pounds of.	Dew-rotted hemp, tons of.	Water-rotted hemp, tons of.	Flax, pounds of.	Flaxseed, bushels of.	Silk cocoons, pounds of.	Maple sugar, pounds of.	Cane sugar, hhds. of 1,000 pounds.	Molasses, gallons of.	Honey and beeswax, pounds of.	Value of home-made manufactures.

SCHEDULE No. 6.—SOCIAL STATISTICS.

Name of town, county, or city.	Aggregate valuation of real and personal estate.	Aggregate amount of taxes assessed.	Public schools.	PUBLIC LIBRARIES.			PERIODICALS, INCLUDING NEWS PAPERS.			
					Number.	Volumes	Name.	Class.	How often published.	Number of circulation.
	Real estate........ $ Personal estate... Total........ How valued. True valuation... $	State .... $ County....... Parish....... Town .... Total.... Road tax..... $ How paid.	Number of colleges........ Number of academies..... Number of free schools... Number of other schools.. Number of school-houses. Amount of money raised by tax for schools last year.. $ Raised in other ways for schools last year........ Received from public funds for schools last year.....	Social.......... Colleges........ Academies....... Public schools.. Sunday schools.						

SCHEDULE No. 6.—SOCIAL STATISTICS—Continued.

Seasons.	Public paupers.	Criminals.	Cost of labor.	Religious worship.
Has this season produced average crops? What crops are short? To what extent? What is the average per year?	Whole number of paupers supported during the past year? Number supported on the 1st day of June. Native { White. Black. Foreign. Cost of supporting paupers during last year.	Number convicted of crime during year ending June 1, 1850. In prison on the 1st June, 1850. Native { White. Black. Foreign.	Average wages to farm hand per month, hired by the year and boarded.......................... $ Average wages of a day laborer— Without board................. With board................. Average payment to a carpenter per day, without board.............. Average wages to a female domestic per week, with board .... Average price of board to a laboring man per week.................	Number of churches. Number of persons each will accommodate. Value of churches.

SCHEDULE No. 5.—PRODUCTS OF INDUSTRY.

Name of corporation, company, or individual producing articles to the annual value of $500.	Name of business, manufacture, or product.	Capital invested in real and personal estate in the business.	Raw material used, including fuel.			Kind of motive power, machinery, structure, or resource.	Average number of hands employed.		Wages.		Annual product.		
			Quantities.	Kinds.	Values.		Male.	Female.	Average monthly cost of male labor.	Average monthly cost of female labor.	Quantities.	Kinds.	Values.

SCHEDULE No. 3.—PERSONS WHO DIED DURING THE YEAR ENDING JUNE 1, 1850.

Name of every person who died during the year ending June 1, 1850, whose usual place of abode at the time of his death was in this family.	Description.				Married or widowed.	Place of birth, naming the State, Territory, or country.	The month in which the person died.	Profession, occupation, or trade.	Disease, or cause of death.
	Age.	Sex.	Color—white, black, or mulatto.	Free or slave.					

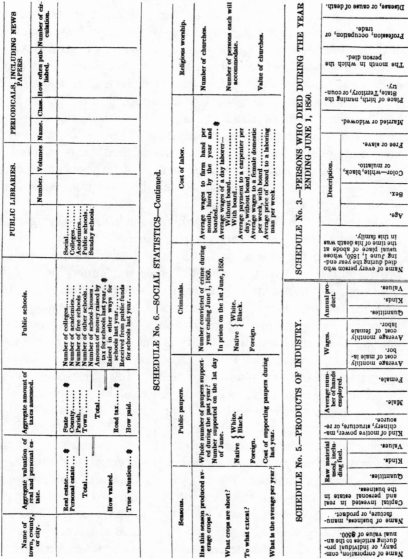

SOURCE: U.S. Bureau of the Census, *The Seventh Census of the United States:* 1850 (Robert Armstrong, printer, Washington, D.C., 1853), xii.

detailed censuses in New York to a complete void in Pennsylvania, a colony in which no enumeration occurred prior to independence. Scattered documents also exist for Spanish and French settlements that eventually were incorporated into the United States.

The second period of census taking began with the Constitution of 1787, which required a count of American citizens every ten years in order to apportion both representation in the House of Representatives in the national Congress and any direct taxes that Congress chose to levy on the states. The first such enumeration was taken in 1790, and a census has followed every ten years. As is evident in Table I, the censuses became increasingly elaborate, although only the heads of families were listed by name. From 1790 to 1840, the family or household was the primary unit of study. Thus, a fair amount is known about such general characteristics of the total population as age, sex, and race. However, detailed analysis of the population cannot be pursued through these documents, and they offer little explanation of why changes were taking place.

The year 1850 marked a major turning point in census taking under the federal government. In that year, the name of every free individual was entered in the census, and a great deal more information was provided for the individuals so listed. People, not families, became the basic unit of investigation, although considerable data were also collected for households and communities. As a result, demographic historians are able to provide much more extensive and sophisticated analysis about the population history of this country after 1850 than before. Note, however, that the published census volumes provide only aggregate data for large numbers of people. However, the actual lists drawn up by the enumerators generally are available to researchers for those censuses taken up through 1900, except for the 1890 census which was almost totally destroyed by a fire. These name-by-name entries can be used for a great deal of in-depth analysis. Similar information is not yet available for more recent counts in the twentieth century because it has been the policy of the Census Bureau to protect the privacy of individuals who are still alive. On the other hand, states such as Iowa, Kansas, New York, Oregon, and Rhode Island also began counting their inhabitants in the middle of the nineteenth century. Because these state counts were usually taken between the national censuses, it is possible to find out a great deal of information for some parts of the United States by using both federal and state sources.

The other major source of demographic data is vital statistics, that is, records of births, deaths, and marriages. In some countries, inhabitants must also register any change of residence, though the United States is not one of them. Our government has collected data on immigration into this country since 1820. Movement out of the country was the subject of data collection only much later. Although there is no register of migration within the country, data from the censuses can be used to study patterns of internal migration in rather close detail.

Similar to the censuses, vital statistics from the American past vary considerably both in origin and in the amount of information they provide. In the seventeenth and eighteenth centuries, vital statistics were collected by both churches and towns, although in New England the distinction was not always clear. For an example of one such list see Table III, which presents the vital events of people connected to the Congregational Church in Plymouth, Massachusetts, in 1763 and 1805. Note that here, as in many church records, baptisms are recorded instead of births! In the twentieth century, the federal government collects most vital statistics, making use of state and local administrative units as places for registering births, deaths, and marriages. The most limited vital statistics provide totals of the numbers of each kind of event that occur in one year. These can be used to calculate the rates of birth, death, and marriage per 1,000 in the population if one knows the population size. Such data provide only the most limited insights into the how and why of demographic change.

TABLE III. PLYMOUTH CHURCH RECORDS, 1763 AND 1805

SOURCE: New England Society in the City of New York, *Plymouth Church Records: 1620–1859,* 2 vols. (New York: The University Press, 1920–1923), I, 393, 454, 493; II, 606, 631, 646. Reprinted with permission of the New England Society in the City of New York.

1763

BAPTISMS

March	20th	Barlett Abig^{l} Daught^{r} of Eben^{r} & Abigail Bartlett
April	3^{d}	Cotton Sarah Daught^{r} of Mr John & Mrs Hannah Cotton
		Churchill Hannah D^{r} of Jonathan & Hannah Churchill
June	19th	Russell Mercy Daught^{r} of John & Mercy Russell
		Faunce Jerusha Daught^{r} of Thomas & Sarah Faunce
July	3^{d}	Torrey Daniel Son to Nathl & Anne Torrey
Augst	21	Churchill Bath^{a} Daug^{r} to Benjn & Ruth Churchill
Sep^{r}	11th	Morton Oliver Son to Silas & Martha Morton
Nov^{r}	13th	Churchill Mercy Daught^{r} of Eben^{r} & Churchill
Dec^{r}	11th	Sproutt Samuel Son to Ebenez^{r} Sproutt & Wife — Middleboro
Dec^{r}	25	Harlow Allice Daught^{r} of Jabez & Exper^{ce} Harlow

Marriages

Jan^{r}	27th	James Holmes Junr & Remember Wetherhead — Ponds
March	24th	Elijah Morey & Rebecca West — Ponds
April	7th	Isaac Mackey & Sarah Harlow
April	28	Josiah Finney Junr & Alice Barns
Sep^{r}	15	Joseph Warren & Mercy Torrey
Oct^{r}	20	Rufus Ripley & Mary Shurtleff
Oct^{r}	27	Joseph Holmes & Phebe Bartlett
Nov^{r}	10	Amos Jeffery & Phebe Sepit (Indians)
Nov^{r}	13th	Judah Bartlett & Love Sprague

Deaths

Jan^{y}	21	Mr Josh^{a} Bramhall
Feb^{r}	19	Samuel Marshall
	24	Capt JnoDouglass
March	1	Asa Beal's Wife, Rhoda
	5th	John King's Wife
	14	Hannah Cooper, Jn^{os} Wid^{w}
	24	Capt Josiah Mort^{ns} Wid^{w}
	30	Doc^{t} LeBarons Negr^{o} Child
Ap^{l}	2^{d}	Saml Clark Aged 76
	12th	James Howard
May	29	Levi Drew's[1] Child
June	29	Wid^{w} Hannah Jackson 82
July	6th	Deac^{n} Torreys Child
	31	Saml Jacksons Child
Aug^{t}	19	Eben^{r} Ryders Child
	25	Revd Alex^{d} Cumming of Bost^{n} Pastor of ye Old South Aged 37
Sep^{r}	6	Benj. Bartletts Child
	12	Nathl Donham Sadler
	16	A French Man
	18	Patience Harlow
	29	Thos Silvesters Wife
	30	Elisha Mortons Child
Oct^{r}	5	Th^{s} Trasks Child
	15	Barn^{s} Hedge's Child
	19	Esqr Winslow's Negr. Child
	20	Wid^{o} Eleanor Holmes 84
	28	Wife [2] of Eleaz^{r} Stephens [3]
Nov^{r}	15	Widow Mercy Tinkam
Dec^{r}	9th	Abigail Hedge Maid^{n}
	29	James Thomas's Child

1805

Baptisms

Jan.	15	Edwin son of Ichabud Morton Jun
March	3	Hannah Poor daughter of James & Sarah Kendall

		Lucy daughter of Peabody & Lucy Bartlett
		Eleazer Stevens Son of Freeman Bartlett
April	28	Sarah Palmer daughter of Lem^{l} Brown[2]
		Lucy daughter of Nathl Holmes
June	30	Mary Dyer / Martha Cotton — children of Joseph & Martha Holmes
July	28	Richard Son of Henry & Mary Warren
		Sarah daughter of Thos Witherell Jun
Aug^{t}	18	Martha Harlow daughter of Benjn Whiting
Sept	29	Lucy Goodwin an adult daughter of Timothy Goodwin
Dec.	1	Maria daughter of Ichabud Morton Jun

Marriages

Jan.	3	John Harlow Jun & Betsey Harlow Torrey both of Plymouth
Feb.	17	George Sylvester & Mary Landman both of Plymouth
March	23	John Goodwin & Deborough Barnes both of Plymouth
	26	Daniel Clark & Martha Bramhall both of Plymouth
April		John Burgis Jun Susanna Sampson both of Plymouth
March	28th	Capt George Drew & Miss Fanny Glover both of Plymouth
April	25	Mr Thomas Jackson & Miss Sarah Le Baron both of Plymouth [176] 1805
May	5	Mr Joshua Bartlett & Miss Elizabeth Goodwin both of Plymouth 100
June	10	Mr. Wm Nye of Sandwich & Miss Lucy Sylvester of Plymouth
July	10	Capt Jesse Harlow & Sally Cotton both of Plymouth
Sep^{r}	8th	John Gray Jun of Kingston & Sarah Battles of Plymouth
Nov.	28	Joseph Wright & Lucy Burgis both of Plym^{o}
		Thomas Fish Jun of Pembroke & Cynthia Doten of Plym^{o}
		John Hall & Mary Pigsley both Plym^{o}
		Wm Leonard & Susanna Bartlett both of Plymouth
Dec.	16	James Curtis of [1] Pembroke & Sarah Churchill of Plymouth
	30	Alpheus Richmond & Abigail Simmonds both of Plymouth

Deaths

Jan^{y}	15	Nehemiah Ripley aged 73
Jan.	18	Sarah Cobb aged 58
	21	Nehemiah Burbank's child aged 2 months
	23	Capt Jesse Harlow's wife aged 66
	26	Wid. Elizth Rider aged 84
Feb.	1	Capt Andrew Farrel - an Irishman resident in Boston who with ten others was shipwrecked on Plymouth Beach on the night of ye 28th of Jany all of whom excepting the first mate perished in the storm.
Feb.	10	John Doten's infant child aged 3 weeks
	12	Rose's daughter a black girl aged 8 years
	23	Widow Sarah Morton aged

26	John Doten's wife aged 24 years
March 11	Wid. Dorothy Bartlett aged
April 5	Wid. E. Brewster's child aged 18 months
6	Jabez Doten aged
9	Nehemiah Cobb aged 51 years
19	Mary Dyer aged 25 years
22	Wm Barnes child aged 18 months
May 18	Polden aged
June 4	Sylvanus Paty's child aged 7 years
5	Josiah Finney's wife aged 37 years & an infant child a week before
June 15	Thomas Monton's 4th child aged
June[1] 5	A child of Richard Holmes Jun. aged 1 year
6	Sylvanus Rogers Child aged 18 months
July	Richard Austin aged
16	Ephraim Harlow's Wife aged 35
July 22	Grandchild of Willard Sears aged 8 years
28	Capt Wm Weston's Wife aged 69 years
Augt 11	Saml Holmes Child aged one year
6	Daniel Churchill's child aged 10 months
19	Mr Bosworth's child aged 4 years
Augt 23	Dr R. Cotton's child aged 16 months
27	Capt. Nathl Holmes aged
31	San^{l} Bradford's child aged
Sep^{t} 6	Atwood Drew's child aged 17 months
	Ansel Holmes child aged 21 months
Sept 30	Capt Cornish's Child aged 3 years
Sept 26	Lydia Holmes aged 37 years
Oct. 3	Charles Ripley's Child aged 20 months
4	Spear's Child aged 13 months
8	Wm Morton aged
9	Calvin Crombie's child aged 20 months
Nov. 26	Joseph Treble aged 75 years
27	Rebecca Dewy aged 60 years
Dec 31	Isaac Barnes child aged 3 years
Nov.	Capt Wm Straffin on his passage to the W. Indies

In order to provide truly sophisticated analysis of the patterns of demographic history, it is necessary to have vital statistics with additional information. For example, birth records that include the age of the mother offer opportunities for much more extensive analysis about patterns of childbearing, and can even be used to determine whether or not deliberate efforts to control family size were practiced by a particular group. A record of an individual's death is much more useful if it includes some indication of the cause of death, the personal characteristics of the deceased such as age or sex, where the individual died, and where the individual resided. Ideally, marriage records should include not only information about the husband and wife but also about their parents. The best records note the ages and the occupations of the husband and wife and their parents, as well as their place of residence.

It is possible to undertake complex analysis for the twentieth century, and especially after the mid-1930s when federal registration of births and deaths became relatively complete. Such studies may include examining childbearing patterns or causes of death depending on the age, sex, race, occupation, and place of residence of the individuals involved. Curiously, nineteenth century vital statistics are relatively poor and have provided only a minimum amount of information for demographic historians.

In contrast, a surprising amount is known about local populations before 1800, thanks to studies based on vital statistics from church and town records. Using the local records, it has been possible to piece together families, and from a large number of families to provide aggregate pictures of rather detailed demographic patterns. Figure 1 shows an actual form used by the author to reconstruct eighteenth- and early nineteenth-century Quaker families from New Jersey records similar to those of the Plymouth Church. In some communities, it has been possible to link this information with data from tax lists, wills, or deeds to provide much more extensive information about demographic patterns depending on the wealth or occupation of people under study. Obviously, the construction of families and placing them in their community requires sufficient information about individuals to successfully establish links from one record to another. This is especially important prior to 1800, when families or towns often contained several individuals of the same name. This author once encountered a death record for a Mary Shotwell at a time when there were over ten women and girls with that name. In the absence of additional information about age, residence, or family tie, such records must be used with caution.

This type of work is extraordinarily time consuming but it does provide remarkable detail about both the population and selected families within particular communities or religious groups. For example, it is possible to determine whether a child in the eighteenth century could expect to marry by birth order, that is the fourth child marrying after the third child had married but before the fifth child. Or one can calculate the number of months between births, perhaps with an interest in determining whether the length of birth interval changes depending on whether the previous child lived, or died before reaching

Figure 1. New Jersey Quaker family reconstructed from vital statistics.

HARNED — Jonathan — Son of: Nathaniel / Annah
Husband

LAING — Sarah — Daughter of: Jacob / Sarah
Wife

MARRIAGE
July 23, 1766
Date of
Jan. 13, 1814
End of Union
47
Length

HUSBAND
1 | 22
Rank | Age at
Ap. 18, 1744
Born
Jan. 13, 1814
Died
69 | Age 69
End of Union | at Death

WIFE
1 | 18
Rank | Age at
May 29, 1748
Born
July 10, 1821
Died
65 | Age 73
End of Union | at Death

Age Group	Yr. Mar.	No. Bir.	Age Moth.	Bir. Int.	CHILDREN Sex	Rank	Birth Date
15-19	2	1	19	12.5	M	1	Aug. 10, 1767
20-24	5	2	21	23	M	2	July 9, 1769
25-29	5	2	23	26	M	3	Sept. 30, 1771
30-34	5	2	25	26	F	4	Dec. 5, 1773
35-39	5	1	27	24	M	5	Dec. 5, 1775
40-44	5	2	32	60	F	6	Dec. 12, 1780
45-49	✓		34	27	M	7	Mar. 16, 1783
Total		10	37	34	F	8	Jan. 17, 1786
Boys		6	40	29	F	9	June 16, 1788
Girls		4	43	40	M	10	Oct. 10, 1791
						11	
						12	
						13	
						14	
						15	
						16	
						17	

Remarks:
* may be Maince a widow of John Harned died 1849
→ 1. yes, he remarried

Born at	Residing at	Place of Marriage
	Middlesex	#094 (9)
	Middlesex	Plainfield

Death Date	Stat.	Age.	Marriage Date	Age	Name	Spouse (last name)
Oct. 23, 1825	M W̄	58		c	David	
Sept. 5, 1828	M	59		c	Jacob	
Jan. 12, 1774	S	2y 3m	———	c	Nathaniel	
		99.0		c	Sarah	
Jan. 17, 1808	W M̄	32	Ap. 25, 1804	28	Nathaniel	Miller (202)
Dec. 17, 1846	M W̄	66	Oct. 28, 1813	32	Anna	ROGERS (233)
Feb. 14, 1848	W* M̄	64	Mar. 27, 1811	28	John	~~—~~ +1 LAING (231)
Mar. 27, 1864	S	78	———		Rebecca	
Dec. 6, 1861	W	73	Mar. 27, 1817	28	Deborah	VAIL (242)
Oct. 25, 1862		71	Oct. 24, 1816	25	Jonathan	married Dalson 1830 WEBSTER (241)

SOURCE: Author's original.

six months of age. For some groups, genealogists have already assembled the data according to families so that an historian can make use of records that have already been provided in their most useful form. It is important to keep in mind, however, that studies of early American communities generally tell us about those people who stayed within the community. Individuals or families who moved away disappear from the records. Considering that Americans have always been a mobile people, it is important to keep in mind that those who moved may well have experienced different demographic patterns than those who stayed.

Censuses and vital statistics are only a part of the wide variety of sources available to demographic historians willing to make use of elaborate and sophisticated techniques of analysis from a variety of disciplines. Some of this additional information provides further insights on basic demographic behavior or the structure of populations. A number of examples will be discussed in the following chapters. Tax lists offer evidence not only about the size of the population but may also indicate variations of demographic behavior according to economic class. In the nineteenth century, many cities published directories listing the heads of households and other individuals living in the community. These directories often were published on a yearly basis. They can be used to determine not only who lived where within the city, but also how long individuals remained within a community and how many new faces appeared in a town in any given year.

An important source of information about past patterns of death comes from what were known in the eighteenth century as "bills of mortality." A bill of mortality is a table of the deaths that occurred in a community in a particular year or period of years, often arranged to indicate the ages of those individuals who died, what time of year mortality was most common, and what the main causes of death were, subject to the limits of medical knowledge at the time. In the nineteenth century, concerns for finding ways to provide better health led to what were known as "sanitary surveys" in a number of cities and states. These were general studies about the health and well-being of communities, and obviously shed considerable light on mortality patterns. Wills might appear to be of use in studying death in the past, but they are often more informative about the number of children to be provided for, whether or not a wife was present, whether she was a first or second wife, and perhaps even some expectation about how long she might live.

Even more exotic sources include gravestones, skeletal remains, archeological evidence of communities, maps, and ships lists of immigrants crossing the Atlantic or slaves being transported from the Chesapeake to the Gulf states. The use of this information can be obvious or extraordinarily imaginative. For example, one set of ships lists of slaves who were being carried from the Chesapeake to the Gulf coast included information about the height and age of those slaves. This has been used to estimate the diet and health of slaves by determining at what ages and how fast growth occurred among adolescent blacks. Tree rings have been studied in order to determine possible changes in the climate that eventually affected the health of a community through both agricultural productivity and the presence or absence of insect-born epidemics.

As scholars have realized the importance of studying the values attached to various demographic events, and have been interested in exploring to what extent values actually determined that behavior, they have increasingly turned to more traditional literary sources. Personal documents, including such familiar items as travel journals, diaries, correspondence, and account books, provide a great deal of information about the diet, clothing, medical practice, and even the extent of birth control in earlier populations. Court records offer insights into family arrangements, including how often orphans had to be provided for and the extent of foster care needed.

Works written for public consumption offer information on a wide variety of topics. In the nineteenth century, manuals were published offering men and women advice regarding marriage, sex, and birth control. Health care and patterns of death were discussed in sources ranging from journals of medical societies, to advice books written by doctors at the time, to advertisements for medicines or services (including abortion) that were published in the newspapers of the time. Newspapers also published accounts of epidemics. Law codes can be used to explore restrictions on migration, marriage patterns, medical practice, and inheritance. By the middle of the nineteenth century, individuals regularly wrote books and articles concerned explicitly with matters of population. In some cases, public debates revolving around demographic issues ranging from westward expansion and the encouragement of immigration to concerns to limit abortion and the spread of birth control information appear in legislative records. Because of this awareness of change, Americans often wrote about them, with both sophistication and passion. They did not, however, always completely understand how far and in what direction the changes would go.

Who Is a Demographic Historian?

Obviously, to do basic research in all aspects of demographic history, especially if one is interested in comparing the findings about his or her own nation to similar patterns elsewhere in the world, is well beyond the capacity of any one human being. In the author's own work on American demographic history he has had occasion to refer to the efforts of actuaries, anthropologists, archeologists, biologists, demographers, economists, geographers, medical men and women, meteorologists, political scientists, psychologists, sociologists, statisticians, and historians whose interests are not necessarily oriented toward population.

In his introduction to his book, *Historical Demography,* T. H. Hollingsworth once described the individual who would seek to understand the history of past populations as follows:

> The ideal historical demographer will need to have a keen historical sense and a command of all the knowledge and resources of modern demography, requiring a thorough acquaintance with the methods and findings of every national system of census and vital registration in the world. He will be deeply versed in economics, sociology, religious observance, archaeology, anthropology, climatology, epidemiology, and gynaecology; and he will understand the mathematical techniques of the statistician so well that he can advance improvements on them of his own. He will be a good palaeographer, an expert on taxation law and practice, on town planning and agricultural methods, at all times and places; he will know how to collect quantitative information, to code and punch it on cards or tapes, and to produce an analysis of it by computer. He will be a voracious reader, with a command of at least a dozen languages, reading a hundred issues of learned periodicals and as many books, emanating from every part of the world, from cover to cover every year.
>
> The ideal historical demographer, of course, does not exist.

A careful reader will no doubt have noticed that Hollingworth writes about historical demography, but this author refers to demographic history. Is there a difference? The answer seems to be yes, though the distinction may be in shades of gray rather than black and white. Historical demographers are interested primarily in the details of past populations and in the demographic processes that produced the observed patterns. They are demographers working with old records. Demographic historians share many of the same interests, but ask additional questions about the social, political, and economic causes and consequences of population patterns. They are, at heart, historians who want to describe and explain why it mattered that demographic characteristics existed in one form and not another. They see the study of fertility and mortality, of size and distribution, of age and sex as necessary, but not sufficient parts of our understanding of the past.

Anyone who would work in the field of demographic history must recognize immediately that interdisciplinary efforts are essential. The demands of basic research require specialization in areas ranging from the statistical manipulation of demographic data to sensitive readings of literary materials that may shed light on the meanings and causes of the patterns of birth, death, or marriage. However, specialists must have an appreciation for, rather than a rejection of, the work of others. Demographic history is most exciting when it ranges widely over much of human experience rather than focusing on questions of limited interest. Because the central issue of both demographic history and demography is the transition over the past two hundred years in patterns of birth, death, marriage, and migration, the link between history and demography is understandable. Demography is, by nature, an historically oriented social science. At the same time, the course of history frequently has been shaped by population patterns. However, a full understanding of demographic history goes well beyond the interaction of history and demography to include most of the disciplines represented in a modern university.

Chapter 2

Revolutions in Childbearing in Nineteenth-Century America

The Subject and Its Interest

The dramatic decline in childbearing, which occurred in the United States between 1800 and 1920, is a subject that has attracted the attention of numerous scholars from different disciplines. The extraordinary nature of the decline is enough to explain at least part of the interest in the topic. The data in Table IV, and in Table V and Figure 2 on page 49, describe the change in detail. Most important, however, is that this revolution in childbearing occurred in a little more than a century. In 1800, the yearly birth rate of the population stood in the neighborhood of 55 births per 1,000 living Americans. By 1920, the birth rate was about half as great in each year.

The birth rate is only one way to describe the frequency of childbearing. Different measures of fertility show only slightly different rates of decline, but the overall pattern remains reassuringly the same. The bottom part of Table IV, in which the level of childbearing in a given year is presented as a proportion of the figure for 1800, shows that by 1820 childbearing among white Americans was about 95 percent as high as it had been in 1800. By the middle of the nineteenth century, the level of fertility was about 75 percent of what it had been earlier; by 1900, fertility had declined to just over half what it had been at the start of the century. In 1930, it was little more than a third of what it had been in 1800. Fertility continued to decline until about 1933 when the long-term decline finally came to a temporary halt. A study by Frederick Crum of the childbearing experience of over twelve thousand wives shows a similar trend. Women who married around 1800, and had their children at the start of the nineteenth century, averaged about 6.4 children. Those who married between 1800 and 1849 had slightly smaller families, averaging 4.9 children and women who married between 1870 and 1879 had only 2.8 children on average.

The various measures of fertility included in the tables and text in

Table IV. American Fertility Rates, 1800–1970

Year	White Birth Rate[a] (1800–1970)	White Total Fertility Rate[b] (1800–1960)	Children 0–4 per 1,000 Women 15–44[c] (White)	(Black)
1800	55.0	7.0	952	—
1810	54.3	6.9	953	—
1820	52.8	6.7	905	810
1830	51.4	6.6	835	830
1840	48.3	6.1	797	785
1850	43.3	5.4	659	741
1860	41.4	5.2	675	724
1870	38.3	4.6	610	692
1880	35.2	4.2	586	759
1890	31.5	3.9	517	621
1900	30.1	3.6	508	582
1910	29.2	3.4	484	519
1920	26.9	3.2	471	429
1930	20.6	2.5	386	393
1940	18.6	2.2	—	—
1950	23.0	3.0	—	—
1960	22.7	3.5	—	—
1970	17.4	—	—	—
		Ratio of 1800 to Later Years		
1800	100	100	100	—
1820	96	96	95	100
1850	79	77	69	92
1870	70	66	64	85
1900	55	51	53	72
1920	49	46	49	53
1930	37	36	41	49
1950	42	43	—	—
1970	32	—	—	—

SOURCES: (a) U.S. Bureau of the Census, *Historical Statistics of the United States, Colonial Times to 1970, Bicentennial Edition* (Government Printing Office, Washington, D.C., 1975), 49; (b) Ansley J. Coale and Melvin Zelnik, *New Estimates of the Fertility and Population in the United States* (Princeton, N.J.: Princeton University Press, 1963), 36; (c) Warren S. Thompson and P. K. Whelpton, *Population Trends in the United States* (New York: McGraw-Hill, 1933), 263.

this chapter fall into two broad categories. The first are often referred to as period measures because they attempt to present the frequency of childbearing at a particular moment in time. Such measures include the birth rate, which indicates the number of births in a year per 1,000 people in the total population. Fertility ratios or child/woman ratios are very similar, but generally indicate the number of children under a given age (five, ten, and sixteen are often used) to the number of women of childbearing age, generally considered to include the years fifteen to forty-five. A second way to measure childbearing is by generation or cohort. Such indices try to determine how many children will replace the previous generation. The average family size at the end of childbearing and "total fertility," which indicates how many children an average woman would have if she married at fifteen and lived with her husband until she was at least forty-five, are two such measures. Any basic text book in demography should allow readers to pursue the specific differences among these and other more refined measures of fertility.

The extraordinary decline in fertility during the nineteenth century should in and of itself attract the attention of numerous scholars. However, it is obvious that such a decline must have had significant effects not only on the families involved but also for American society as a whole. In studying this decline, it is important to remember that Americans were not the only people to reduce their childbearing in the nineteenth century. Many of the nations of western Europe experienced a similar change in childbearing, though the time at which the change began and the degree of decline frequently differ significantly from the pattern observed in the United States. The important point to remember, however, is that increased fertility control was not unique to the United States, and to fully understand it may eventually require comparing the experience of Americans to that of the English, French, German, and other Europeans.

There are, however, some aspects of the American patterns that require special attention. For example, although the decline in fertility was widespread in western Europe and in the United States, Americans began to control their childbearing earlier than any other group of people, except perhaps the French. Americans actually began to limit the size of their families as much as a century before similar changes are observable in some European nations. In addition, the American birth rate was far higher than that found in most European countries at the end of the eighteenth and in the early nineteenth centuries. In the United States, the birth rate was over 50 per 1,000; a comparable figure for many European populations was probably in the neighborhood of 35 per 1,000. In spite of the fact that the United

States was not the only nation to experience a dramatic reduction in childbearing, our attention here will be limited to the American experience.

Since the 1930s, the American population has experienced some dramatic fluctuations in childbearing. In the middle of the 1930s, the long-term decline in fertility came to an end and the birth rate fluctuated slightly until about 1940. Then the birth rate began to rise slowly, with more dramatic increases coming after World War II. The so-called "baby boom" typified the late 1940s and much of the 1950s. After 1957, the birth rate once again dropped significantly, although in recent years it has begun to edge upward slightly. Whether this recent upturn is a revival of higher levels of fertility, or is merely a small echo of the post-World War II baby boom, is not at present clear. Nonetheless, fertility patterns of the American population since the 1930s have been characterized by dramatic fluctuations both in the scale and the abruptness of the turnaround. However, this chapter will focus primarily on the nineteenth century experience; changes in fertility from 1920 on will receive only marginal attention.

Such dramatic changes in the level of childbearing would no doubt have attracted the attention of historical demographers eventually. However, the story is complex enough and is related to enough different aspects of American social history to have generated widespread interest among other scholars as well.

One of the first groups to be concerned with the reduction in childbearing were the people who were curious about the possible effects of widespread immigration on the American population. As early as 1843, a Virginian named George Tucker observed that immigrants seemed to have larger families than native-born Americans. Eight years later, Jessie Chickering, a Massachusetts resident, made similar observations. Neither drew ominous conclusions from their observations, although both found them extremely interesting. However, later commentators on this subject began to express fears that the American population was being transformed in alarming ways. In the early years of the twentieth century, President Theodore Roosevelt and Charles W. Eliot, president of Harvard University, spoke publically of "race suicide." By this they meant that the native white population seemed to be reducing its childbearing level below replacement when confronted with hordes of new immigrants from abroad. These men feared that ultimately the native-born population of the United States, which they considered to be superior to the new immigrants, would eventually be replaced by people whom they felt to be inferior.

The result of these comments was a series of studies by Frederick

Crum, Carl Jones, and others designed to see whether or not these fears were real. Studies of genealogies of native, white American families revealed, much to the alarm of many old-line Americans, that in fact childbearing had been falling during the nineteenth century. The concern with the fertility differentials between native, white Americans and immigrants continued into the 1930s. Since then, restrictions on immigration by law, the Great Depression, and World War II, and the gradual reduction of childbearing among the more recent arrivals have reduced this source of interest in fertility control.

After World War II, a new source of interest in the fertility decline emerged. Since 1950, concern with the worldwide population explosion has generated interest in whether or not the demographic transition, by which European and American populations reduced both their death and birth rates to levels much lower than had existed in the eighteenth century, would be repeatable elsewhere. Many scholars believe that the historic transition must be repeated in the rest of the world otherwise the population explosion will eventually overwhelm the resources of the earth. Within the context of this interest the United States experience was especially fascinating, in part because the American transition had begun at a time when the country was still largely rural, a condition that is common in many parts of Asia, Africa, and Latin America. In contrast, many European nations did not experience the demographic transition until they had achieved significant levels of urbanization and industrialization.

One important result of this post-World War II interest in childbearing patterns was to move beyond simple descriptions of the nineteenth century decline, which had been sufficient to confirm the fears of early twentieth-century Americans about the possibility of "race suicide," to consider questions of how, and ultimately why, declines in childbearing have occurred. Questions of motive and technique are especially important if we are to predict whether such declines in childbearing will ultimately occur elsewhere in the world or whether the population explosion will come to an end through increases of mortality caused by widespread ill health and malnutrition.

In the last two decades, historians have joined the sociologists and demographers who first explored the transformation in American childbearing. This can be attributed to at least three different concerns of the new social history, a type of history that focuses on basic aspects of the lives of all people, instead of the public events that involve prominent adult, white males. Scholars interested in the changing role of women in American society have found the decline in childbearing of obvious interest. Comparisons between the childbearing experiences of black and white Americans have been undertaken as one means of testing whether or not black Americans have shared similar experiences as whites, or whether their life in the United States has been dramatically different. Historians whose primary interest was in the structure and functioning of families in nineteenth-century America soon realized that, whatever their initial interest, they had to understand the dramatic effects that demographic changes had on American families during the nineteenth and twentieth centuries. Conversely, the impact of family life on demographic changes must also be studied, because American families are traditionally the locus in which most individuals experience such basic life events as birth, death, marriage, and even migration. Thus, families were tied to demographic change in complex links of cause and effect.

Even new social historians, whose concern is primarily with politics and the balance of power within American society, have found these demographic changes of vital concern to them. One source of their interest revolves around the simple question of whether or not large numbers of Americans have been passive respondents to social forces or were actively in control of their own lives. One way to study this particular question is to examine how the birth rate declined in the nineteenth century. For example, were women, who were frequently portrayed as subject to male authority within their families, controllers of fertility or were they subject to the whims of their husbands in any decision to limit the size of their family? Likewise, were black Americans simply the victims of social forces when they began to have fewer children in the late nineteenth century, or were they actively seeking to reduce their own fertility, much as middle class, white Americans had some fifty years earlier? Was the delay a question of timing related to common factors, or were blacks different in some fundamental way in how they fit into American society?

The Sources and What They Tell Us

One of the first problems confronting students of the nineteenth-century decline in fertility simply was to describe the change. In order to understand exactly how the change occurred, it was necessary not only to be able to define how great the change was but also to locate its origins in time and place. Once this information was available, it could be associated with other changes in American society that might be identified as possible causes. Unfortunately, in the nineteenth century the United States, as a nation, lacked any kind of birth registration system. As a result, lists of births that might have been combined with census figures to calculate annual birth rates are not available. One question of central importance then to the early students of the fertility decline was how to measure it.

Two types of sources are available that provide partial answers to this question. It is worth commenting on the strengths and weaknesses of both types of sources, and on the information each one offers. One type of source is censuses that list individuals by age, and that in some cases actually record the number of children adult women claim to have given birth to. The other is genealogical materials. In some instances, scholars have been able to use actual genealogies; in other instances, students have had to reconstruct families from lists of births, marriages, and deaths found either in community archives or in the records of particular religious groups. Neither type of source nor the information that can be derived from them is entirely accurate or adequate to understanding the decline in childbearing. However, together they provide complementary results that offer a remarkably full and complete understanding of the decline in childbearing, at least in a descriptive sense.

Censuses are useful because they offer wide coverage, allowing students to examine childbearing patterns in all the states and across a long period of time starting in 1800 and running down into the twentieth century. On the other hand, census data are shaped by the questions that the census enumerators asked in a particular year; some of the details about the declines in childbearing are unavailable from these particular sources.

The principal means by which censuses have been used to describe the decline in childbearing is the construction of what is known as a "fertility ratio." Although different scholars have preferred various techniques to construct these ratios, the general process is easily described and elaborates on the definition provided earlier. Using information on the age and sex composition of the population, it is possible, particularly after 1840, when the censuses began to be fuller in their descriptive detail, to construct ratios of the number of children under some age (such as five, ten, or sixteen) in the population to the number of women in the childbearing ages, generally considered to be between fifteen and forty-five. Some scholars prefer one ratio; others, another. But in general, the overall patterns do not vary greatly, regardless of which ratio is used.

The following briefly summarizes the results of studies by scholars such as Yasukichi Yasuba, or Colin Forster and G. S. L. Tucker. Beginning in 1800, fertility ratios can be observed as declining, starting in the northeastern part of the United States and then spreading gradually westward and southward across the country. By 1860, many of the midwestern states, which once had dramatically higher fertility ratios than those in the northeast, showed fertility ratios that were similar to those found in the northeast in earlier decades. However, by the middle of the nineteenth century the northeastern states had continued to experience falling fertility, so they still recorded lower levels of childbearing than did the Midwest. The important point to keep in mind is that, in spite of significant regional differences in any one census year, in the long run fertility declined in all regions of the United States, though the time at which that change began and how fast it occurred did vary from one region to another.

However, there are some significant difficulties in interpreting what reduced numbers of children to women of childbearing age actually means. It is possible that such a decline could occur for reasons unrelated to actual reductions in childbearing. For example, changes in the age distribution of the population could produce such a result. Women between the ages of twenty and twenty-nine have children at more rapid rates than women over the age of thirty. Thus, if in a particular state there was a shift in the age distribution of the population so that women between twenty and twenty-nine became increasingly rare compared to those women between the ages of thirty and thirty-nine, it would be only natural to expect fewer children under the age of five.

Changes in the sex ratio of the population might also influence the fertility ratio calculated from any two censuses. Although the sex ratio itself would not directly affect the results, primarily because the fertility ratio relates the number of children to women only, the sex ratio frequently does influence marriage patterns. A significant reduction in the number of males in a particular state might well have meant that women who otherwise would have married and had children would find themselves living as single women. As a result, the number of children in the population under the age of five would fall, even though married women continued to have children at a relatively rapid rate. Under such conditions, the reduction in the fertility ratio would be the result of fewer married women rather than married women having fewer children.

One other explanation of some significance is the possibility that mortality in the population was rising. In any census the number of children under the age of five is the result of two interacting phenomena. The first is obviously the number of children born in the previous five years; the other involves the level of mortality which determines how many of them will survive to be counted in the census.

Thus, if mortality rose significantly, from one year to another or from one region to another, the number of children surviving to be counted in the census would decline. As a result, what appears to be a decline in childbearing might simply be a reflection of increasing levels of mortality and fewer children surviving to be counted.

Finally, migration patterns need to be considered as a possible explanation for regional differences in childbearing or differences that can be observed over time. If, as indeed was the case, immigrants had more children than native-born American women, then any state that received significant numbers of immigrants would presumably have unusually large numbers of children recorded by the census. Similarly, as the level of immigration ebbed and flowed, the number of children recorded in a census would also go up and down. Thus, it is important to make sure that declining ratios of children to women of childbearing age actually reflect reductions in childbearing rather than changes in the age distribution, increased mortality, decreased numbers of women marrying, or shifts in the population from primarily native born to primarily immigrant.

Over the last twenty years, scholars have become more sophisticated in handling these problems. This is partly the result of an increasing awareness of these problems, and is partly the result of the development of digital computers that now allow large amounts of data to be manipulated in complex ways that were impractical in the days of rotary calculators. Recent results have shown that changes in population composition, while having some small effect on fertility ratios, by and large do not explain the extraordinary decline that occurred in the nineteenth century. Thus, it can be safely concluded, as Maris Vinovskis has demonstrated, that fertility fell in the first half of the nineteenth century because of efforts on the part of Americans to reduce their childbearing and not because of demographic causes beyond their control. The question of why they chose to reduce their childbearing will be looked at shortly.

As mentioned earlier, genealogies, or lists of births, marriages, and deaths from which families can be reconstructed, offer a second type of material by which to discern whether or not families actually had fewer children over the course of the nineteenth century. Studies using these sources are particularly helpful, in that they provide detailed information about the childbearing patterns of individual families, something that census records generally do not allow us to study. On the other hand, genealogical studies tend to be time consuming, especially if one has to reconstruct the families from the vital statistics records. As a result, such studies tend to focus on relatively small groups. Furthermore, in a particularly mobile society, such as the United States was in the nineteenth century, many family records are lost or at least cannot easily be put together, so that those families for whom we have complete information cannot necessarily be considered to be representative of the American population as a whole. Nonetheless, when results from these records are used in conjunction with fertility ratios derived from censuses they are extremely helpful.

The first efforts to use these materials came in the early twentieth century when men such as Crum, George Engelmann, and Carl Jones sought to determine the substance behind the fears of "race suicide." These studies focused on the childbearing experiences of the native born, white population, and did in fact demonstrate that these groups were having fewer children in each successive generation. More recent studies using similar techniques have their roots in the questions of the new social history, and have been influenced by research on French and English communities. One of the most fascinating results of these kinds of studies has been to demonstrate the complex patterns by which the decline in fertility actually occurred. For example, my work on Quakers in the middle colonies demonstrated that this particular group of Americans began to control their childbearing about the time of the American Revolution. Recently, however, Louise Kantrow has studied elite Quaker families in Philadelphia and has discovered that among this group of prosperous, urban Quakers childbearing did not begin to decline until the first third of the nineteenth century. Presumably these Quakers were not subject to the same pressures that encouraged their rural neighbors to begin to limit their families at a somewhat earlier time. In Nantucket, a commercial fishing area in Massachusetts, Edward Byers discovered that childbearing seems to have been reduced in the latter part of the eighteenth century. On the other hand, studies of Mormon families in the nineteenth century by M. Skolnick and others find that significant reductions in childbearing did not occur until the end of the nineteenth century, when Utah began to be invaded by large numbers of non-Mormons. In fact, Mormon childbearing rates seem actually to have risen in the middle of the nineteenth century. This has been attributed to childbearing among those Mormons who were the first to be raised from childhood in the Mormon faith and who had never experienced significant contact with other groups of Americans. The earliest Mormons had been born and raised in the northeastern parts of the United States, regions in which childbearing was already coming under control when they were converted to the Mormon faith.

Genealogical studies reflect the complex patterns by which

childbearing was reduced in another way. The Quaker couples studied by Wells seem to have had children in an uncontrolled fashion early in their marriages and then, having apparently achieved some overall desired level of family size, tried to control or eliminate all together any future childbearing. In contrast, Jones's New Englanders seem to have limited their family size primarily by increasing the time between births, from approximately every two to two and a half years in the eighteenth century, to a point at which children arrived in a family on the average of every three to four years. Only later did wives in these groups cease having children at ages when they still were physically able to bear offspring.

Eventually, most Americans came to be what are called family planners as opposed to family limiters. The distinction is that family limiters simply seek to reduce the ultimate size of their families. Family planners, on the other hand, wish not only to control the number of children ever born but also the spacing between children. Most American couples have now come to the point where they not only control the length of time between childbearing but also severely restrict the size of the family, so few wives have children beyond their early thirties, a remarkable contrast to the late eighteenth century when women ceased having children only after they had achieved their fortieth birthday. The choices individual members of particular groups made regarding when to begin to limit their childbearing, and whether they curtailed childbearing by attempting to maintain a desired family size or by lengthening the birth interval, are of particular interest because they reflect both on the possible techniques that might have been used to reduce the family size and also on the motives that may have influenced parents to have fewer children.

When the data from studies based on census information are combined with those based on genealogies or vital statistics records, the conclusions are easy to summarize. The general decline in fertility in the nineteenth century was significant; it occurred primarily as a result of family limitation by married couples; and it occurred via a variety of patterns with regard to timing and the specific pattern of control within marriage. Thus, although the dramatic reduction of fertility in the nineteenth century was a general American phenomena, researchers must be careful not to generalize from the experience of one group to another with regard to how, why, or when they chose to limit their children.

Why the Change?

In an age when birth control is almost universally accepted, it is sometimes difficult to remember that the nineteenth-century husbands and wives who deliberately limited the number of children they would have were engaging in truly revolutionary activity. Thus, it is historically important to ask the question of why the couples involved would wish to have fewer children. This question is important whether one is interested in nineteenth-century American social history or the possibility of a similar decline in fertility among today's high fertility populations. The answers regarding possible motives for the control of childbearing are many and varied, ranging from those stressing effects of economic and social changes on large groups, to those that emphasize individual choices confronting women and men of the nineteenth century. The results also reflect the perspectives of students from many different disciplines.

1. Ethnic and Racial Differences

It is difficult to sort out the causes behind the decline in fertility completely. From Ira Rosenwaike's study of New York or Tamara Hareven's and Maris Vinovskis's work on Boston, we know that Irish, Italians, Germans, and black and white Americans all had different rates of childbearing. But how can these differences be explained? For example, differences in the level of childbearing among various ethnic groups may reflect religious teachings regarding the relationship between reproduction and marriage, family preferences rooted in Old World experiences but altered by American realities, differences in infant mortality that might influence parents to have an extra child, or on the contrary to have fewer children, or the fact that ethnicity, class, and occupation are often highly interrelated. Thus, ethnic differences may merely reflect income and occupational differences at work through ethnicity. To be specific, if one were to find that in a particular community Irish immigrants had higher fertility than native born, white Americans, this might not necessarily be the result of the immigrants being Irish, but might reflect the fact that Irish in that particular town were restricted to certain income and occupational groups that frequently engaged in high fertility behavior.

Early scholars were not necessarily aware of these problems, and even when they were, they were faced with the problems of trying to untangle complex webs of cause and effect with data that were limited. In recent years, the advent of computers has made it possible to use complex statistical techniques to sort out some of these relationships. Nevertheless, it is important to recognize that it is still difficult to get the precise information needed to answer these questions. For example, scholars are interested in the impact of education on decisions of whether or not to have an additional child. However, education is a rather general concept and frequently students of the problem are forced to rely on measures such as years of schooling or simple literacy, defined as the ability of an individual to sign his or her name. Needless to say, these measures of education are not as precise as a researcher often requires. On the other hand, they do advance our understanding of fertility control beyond the initial formulations of the problem.

In reviewing the arguments for ethnicity as an explanation for the nineteenth-century fertility decline, it is worth recalling that some of the earliest students of the subject sought to explain this phenomenon by "race suicide." The concept reflected the belief that for some unexplained reason white, Anglo-Saxon, Protestant Americans were unwilling to compete with supposedly inferior immigrant groups in some kind of childbearing race. This is a particularly curious idea to appear at a time when many thought that superior people were justified in seizing the lands of inferior individuals and groups. In addition, it is equally curious that the same Americans who feared the influx of "inferior" immigrants also believed that black Americans, who were considered to be on the bottom of the social order, would not be able to survive a similar competition with their superior white neighbors unless they were somehow or other granted legal protections. Suffice it to say, nobody believes these explanations now, partly because we have moved beyond such blatantly racist views of society and partly because immigrants rather quickly adopted patterns of childbearing that were similar to native white Americans.

2. URBANIZATION

A second explanation for the decline in fertility emerged from the observation that childbearing was frequently reduced in countries and at times when people were also moving into cities. Thus, urbanization in a very general sense came to be used as an explanation. The argument involving urbanization as a cause for declining fertility asserted that families in the cities did not need children as much as farm families simply because they did not need the labor of their children. Also, as infant mortality declined in urban areas in the late nineteenth and early twentieth centuries, couples might decide to have fewer children because they no longer needed to have large families to insure security in their old age.

The detailed studies published during the last two decades have generally undermined this explanation. To begin with, it has been discovered that fertility declined in rural areas, frequently *before* it began to decline in cities, and it also began to decline *before* infant mortality fell. In addition, studies of urban work patterns have found that many children worked in factories or home industries because children's wages were important to the well-being of their families. Thus, it seems unlikely that working class families in urban areas would automatically have any less desire to have children than farm couples, if only because urban environments offered a greater opportunity to profit from the labor of young children than farms where a greater physical size and strength is needed before a child is truly productive. Of course, middle-class families, in which children did not work at all, may have responded according to the traditional explanation. In a few instances, scholars have discovered that fertility actually rose slightly in the early years of urbanization, probably because the wages offered to workers moving into the cities allowed them to marry earlier than they might otherwise have done if they had remained on the farm. A final observation is simply that urbanization is not the same as industrialization. Many individuals who moved into early nineteenth-century cities did not actually work in factories and found themselves engaged in professional or commercial pursuits, construction, or day labor. In addition, in the early nineteenth century, rural areas often were almost as industrialized as their urban neighbors. This is especially interesting because the explanation for why movement into the cities should produce smaller families is really more closely related to work patterns associated with large-scale factories that employed adults for wages rather than anything inherent in residence in a densely settled community.

3. Land Scarcity

One of the most popular and durable explanations for falling family sizes in rural areas involves the relative abundance or scarcity of land. Until the late nineteenth century, land was the principal source of income in American society, which was basically agricultural in its make-up. As early as the middle of the eighteenth century, a Swiss traveler in the American colonies by the name of Peter Kalm and that famous American, Benjamin Franklin, both explained colonial families that were larger than those found in Europe by the relative ease of acquiring farms in the American colonies. Both Kalm and Franklin argued that this enabled young Americans to marry earlier, with the result that they had a longer period of time in which to raise large numbers of children. Given this explanation, it is not surprising that students of the nineteenth-century decline have turned it around to claim that increasingly scarce land produced lower fertility. The links between declines in the availability of land and decreases in childbearing include arguments that population growth might have forced individuals to delay marriage and hence reduced their ability to have large families; as their farms became increasingly smaller, there would have been no need for the labor of large numbers of children; and lower incomes raised the prospect of difficulty in caring for large numbers of children, either when they were small or when they had to be established on their own later in life. Yasuba, and later Forster and Tucker, and Donald Leet are among those who have examined the association between land scarcity and falling family size, showing that at least some of the change in childbearing patterns in nineteenth-century America may be explained in this way. Nonetheless, not all the change can be attributed to this effect, and the precise chain of cause and effect as it worked in individual families in particular communities is difficult to demonstrate.

Special attention can be given to three problems confronting this particular explanation. Scarcity itself is an idea that is difficult to define precisely. Some scholars have simply attempted to relate the density of population in a particular region to the total acreage. A more sophisticated measure of scarcity involves the relative cost of purchasing a farm in a particular community or state. Both, however, are somewhat unsatisfactory, because they do not take into account the quality of the land. Thus, cost (demand) may in fact reflect the relative scarcity of land with regard to the total size of the population, or it may simply indicate that some land is better than other land for purposes of raising crops. A particularly interesting solution to the problem of defining scarcity was Richard Easterlin's effort to relate the number of acres in a particular community farmed in a given year to the maximum number of acres ever farmed in that same community. He then attempted to trace changes in fertility patterns to the ratio of currently utilized acres to total acres ever farmed in the region. Easterlin discovered that as the number of acres in the community being farmed approached the maximum number of acres ever farmed in that region, fertility declined dramatically.

The ways in which the cost of acquiring increasingly scarce land actually lead to the declines in family size are not entirely clear. For example, it may be that young couples confronted with the need to purchase land before they married were forced to delay marriage until they had acquired enough cash to buy a piece of property large enough to sustain a family. On the other hand, the problem may not have been one that emerged before marriage, but may have been related to the fact that some parents felt obliged to help their children get established as they reached marriageable age. In this situation, the cost of setting up farms for one's children would be the inhibiting factor in having large families, instead of the initial cost of establishing one's own farm. In both cases, judgments regarding the cost of land are complicated by expectations regarding standards of living. As standards of living rose during the nineteenth century, it may well be that young men and women were reluctant to start out as poor as their parents had been, so the cost of acquiring a suitable farm would increase simply because children in the middle of the nineteenth century were unwilling to accept the harsh realities involved in getting established earlier in the century. Mid-nineteenth-century Americans may have felt it was necessary to insure a higher income by acquiring more and better property before they married and began to raise children.

A final criticism that can be raised with regard to the land scarcity hypothesis simply notes that while this explanation may be adequate for rural regions, it does nothing to explain why childbearing also fell in urban areas at the same time. Ultimately, any full explanation for the nineteenth-century decline in family size must be able to explain why childbearing was reduced in both rural and urban areas during the nineteenth century.

4. Scarcity in General

An obvious solution to this problem has been to generalize the land scarcity hypothesis to one which explains childbearing choices in terms of general economic abundance or scarcity. According to this model, advanced in various forms by Easterlin and Peter Lindert, prospective parents ask themselves whether or not they can afford to have children at the present time or whether it is advisable to delay having children until their economic prospects are more favorable. This explanation assumes rational choices on the part of very young men and women in the early years of their marriage. It is also based on the assumption that young couples have full information about their long-term earnings and the costs of rearing children as well. In their most sophisticated forms, scarcity theories posit relative judgments about one's economic well-being based on the relationship of the economy when young men and women were growing up to the performance of the economy when they are about to begin childbearing. To take a recent example, Easterlin explained the post-World War II baby boom at least partly as the result of high wages after the war that looked even better than they actually were because many of the people who were earning these wages had been raised during the Great Depression. Thus, the influence of high wages toward large numbers of children was enhanced because of the early childhood experiences of many of the young couples who were beginning to decide how many children they would want.

A critique of the general scarcity model that is particularly telling raises the question of whether people are in fact as rational or as fully informed on their long-term income prospects as the model requires. It is difficult to accept that young men and women in their early twenties have a complete sense of how much they are likely to be earning when they are forty, when their families are likely to be at maximum size and imposing maximum demands on their incomes. In addition, as Easterlin has noted, the general scarcity model is a "notably sexless subject," ignoring the power of passion and the appeal of sex in decisions of whether or not to have children.

Finally, the scarcity model is frequently related to wages earned by the husband or, in the context of the nineteenth century, to the ability of young men to purchase farms. This observation is particularly interesting because, as we shall see later, many nineteenth-century birth control techniques were actually controlled by the wife. Thus, explanations that involve the concerns of males in a marriage may not be adequate when it was their wives who were deciding whether or not to use particular forms of birth control.

5. Occupation and Income

A few studies have offered economic explanations for childbearing decisions in terms of occupation and income instead of relative economic scarcity. One of the most interesting, by Michael Haines, has examined the childbearing patterns of miners and workers in metalurgical industries in both the United States and in Europe. Haines has observed a consistent pattern that crosses national boundaries in which miners and workers in metalurgical industries seem to have had higher fertility than either their rural neighbors or other individuals involved in urban types of economic activity. In addition, Haines's work is interesting because he argues that fertility was not the only demographic pattern that was associated with occupation; migration, marriage, and mortality also seem to have been linked to what people did to earn their livings. Haines's explanation for occupational differences in childbearing is relatively straight forward. He sees miners as having brought to mining communities relatively high fertility values developed in their rural origin. These individuals settled in relatively small towns where they frequently were able to establish small farms or gardens that enhanced an already promising standard of living based on wages that were generally higher than they might have been expected to earn had they remained in the agricultural communities from whence they came. In addition, communities based on coal mining or the production of metals in mills offered few opportunities for employment for wives outside the home, and so fostered early marriage and frequent childbearing. Although this particular study offers us an example in which fertility actually seems to have risen rather than declined, as was more typically the case throughout the nineteenth century, Haines's work does remind us of the necessity to examine differences between groups based on occupation and income, especially when such differences can be separated from the influence of culture.

6. Attitudes and Values

It is important to supplement studies that rely on general economic and social changes to explain reductions in childbearing with works that recognize that ultimately decisions about whether or not to have an extra child were made by individual husbands and wives in the context of their own particular family. This requires understanding the way in which nineteenth-century American couples viewed childbearing. Such an approach demands not only knowledge of how couples perceived children but also an awareness of some of their attitudes about society in general.

Both Maris Vinovskis and I have argued that nineteenth-century America saw the widespread acceptance of a particular cluster of values, often termed modern, which would have encouraged individual men and women to have fewer children when faced with particular types of problems. The argument for this involves two lines of reasoning. First of all, in China and India today, where populations are large and land is relatively scarce, there has been no automatic reaction on the part of people to scarce resources that produces reductions in family size. Before individuals will respond to increasing economic scarcity by seeking to control fertility, they must first perceive large families as problems, and, secondly, must believe they can take actions that will either preserve or improve their economic or social conditions. Attitudes that stress individuals' capacities to know and control their lives, instead of passively having to accept whatever fate or the gods deal out to them, may also have been conducive to other demographic changes during the nineteenth century, such as efforts to control disease or to encourage people to move to new environments, either in the West or in urban areas.

An important recent book by Vinovskis shows that by the time one untangles all of the various interrelated effects of possible declines or increases in mortality, changes in the sex ratio, influxes of immigrants, changing land scarcity, and altered wage patterns, the one variable that may best explain why fertility falls in a community is a measure of education and/or literacy. Where education is high, by and large fertility is relatively low. An association between education and reduced fertility is not too surprising because education itself may be a response to the belief that individuals can make a better life through increased knowledge. In addition, education obviously makes it easier to acquire knowledge about how to limit family size, particularly since many birth-control techniques were described in books published in the middle of the nineteenth century. Furthermore, education, particularly among women, must have increased awareness of and desire for alternatives to a life spent in rearing children. In the eighteenth century, most couples anticipated a minimum of forty years in rearing their children before they were free to pursue their own interests. It is clear that by the mid-nineteenth century women, and probably men as well, were no longer willing to devote such an extraordinarily large proportion of their lives to the process of producing the next generation.

It is only fair to note that a number of scholars are not entirely satisfied with this particular theory. One line of criticism revolves around the effects of education and/or literacy. Literacy and education are obviously not the same thing, and are frequently very difficult to measure. For example, education is frequently measured in terms of years of schooling, with no attention to content or what was actually learned. The most basic measure of literacy has often been the ability to sign one's name, a skill easily mastered by a four-year old, which indicates nothing about the capacity to read either simple or complex material. Furthermore, Harvey Graff has suggested that associations between literacy and other aspects of social change are often more myth than reality when one tries to establish causal connections. Until it can actually be shown that education or literacy actually contributed to an individual's decisions to have fewer children the precise association between the two must remain uncertain.

Other scholars object to the more general concept of modernization. They argue that the idea of modernization, a label often loosely applied to many of the changes that combine to distinguish the twentieth-century world from that of the eighteenth century, is too vague a concept to be useful in explaining as specific a social change as reduced fertility. They point out that an emphasis on values can cause one to overlook powerful changes in prevailing social and economic arrangements that may have forced individuals to change their behavior. In addition, the term "modern" can carry with it implications of superiority that are culturally and politically offensive and can suggest that older forms of behavior were not a matter of choice. Such criticism raises questions about the extent to which large families in the past were conscious and sensible responses to a very different world.

These concerns are obviously valid, but if one is careful to distinguish modern values or personality characteristics from modern institutions such as factories or large-scale political parties, and is careful not to consider this way of looking at the world as necessarily better or worse than alternative sets of values, then the concept continues to have some utility. It is difficult to argue that twentieth-century men and women view the world and their lives in the same way that seventeenth and eighteenth century couples did. It is only reasonable to expect that any change in values and attitudes might well have interacted extensively, as both cause and effect, with the patterns of childbearing that were newly emerging during the nineteenth century. It is not necessary to assume that individuals were either completely modern or completely traditional and passive in their view of world affairs, nor is it necessary to assume that all individuals in America became modern in their outlook at the same time in order to believe that new attitudes were associated with revolutionary behavior. In addition, new values would not necessarily have produced demographic changes in the absence of changes in the social structure (such as, land scarcity, urbanization) that presented nineteenth-century men and women with unfamiliar problems and possibilities. Imaginative efforts to explain the complex causes for the revolution in childbearing will continue to be welcome as we seek to change plausible explanations into proven ones.

Black Childbearing—Similar or Different?

As the outlines of the nineteenth century decline in fertility have become increasingly clear, scholars are demonstrating an interest in those groups whose experience did not parallel the general. As a result, studies involving black fertility have become increasingly important in recent years. A simple outline of black childbearing patterns begins with the observation that at the end of the eighteenth century white and black women seem to have given birth to children at approximately the same rates. However, by the end of the nineteenth century, white women had reduced their fertility significantly from the levels found at the start of the period. In contrast, blacks do not seem to have experienced any significant reduction in childbearing until after 1880 (see Tables IV and V and Figure 2). In 1880, however, black fertility began to drop rapidly, until it was nearly equal to that of their white contemporaries by the 1930s. Since then, black fertility has generally paralleled white childbearing patterns, increasing during the post-World War II baby boom and decreasing after the late 1950s. In spite of the remarkable, overall parallels between white and black childbearing, black fertility has remained above white fertility in every year.

In seeking explanations for why blacks were late in reducing their fertility and why, once they began to have fewer children, their patterns have paralleled the experience of white Americans, a number of interesting issues have been raised, many of them as much political and emotional as demographic.

One explanation is that the parallels observed since 1880 are in fact misleading, and that, as with the rest of their experience with American society, the details of black childbearing are dramatically different. Any parallels, although visible on graphs of childbearing patterns, are accidental; the causes for smaller black families are not the same as the causes for smaller white families. In particular, Reynolds Farley, and Phillips Cutright and Edward Shorter have argued that black Americans have been victims of poor health both in terms of deficient diets from low incomes, and in terms of contracting venereal disease and other genital infections which reduced their capacity to bear children. From this perspective, improved diet that increased maternal health and better medical care that reduced sterility resulting from venereal diseases after the 1930s were responsible for the upturn in black fertility; any parallel upturn in white fertility was entirely coincidental.

Critics of this view, such as Joseph McFalls and George Masnick, claim that there is little or no evidence of a rise in venereal disease after 1880 that would have produced the initial fall in childbearing, and indeed there is no convincing evidence of a subsequent large-scale control of venereal disease in the 1930s. In addition, Edward Meeker has shown that beginning about 1880 black Americans began to be better educated, more highly urbanized, and began to earn better wages, all phenomena that have been associated with the control of fertility among white Americans. Interestingly, when he examined childbearing in various sections of the United States, Meeker

Table V. Crude birthrate and total fertility of the black population, 1850–1969

Interval	Birthrate[a]	Total fertility	Interval	Birthrate[a]	Total fertility
1850-59	58.6[b]	7.90	1920-24	30.1	3.52
1860-69	55.1[c]	7.58	1925-29	27.3	3.17
1870-79	55.4[b]	7.69	1930-34	24.3	2.80
1880-84	51.9	7.26	1935-39	22.9	2.63
1885-89	49.1	6.79	1940-44	24.5	2.83
1890-94	47.1	6.32	1945-49	27.6	3.30
1895-99	45.5	5.85	1950-54	30.6	3.95
1900-04	43.4	5.37	1955-59	31.5	4.38
1905-09	40.1	4.84	1960-64	28.8	4.10
1910-14	36.9	4.38	1965-69	22.8	3.23
1915-19	31.9	3.75			

Note: Crude birthrate refers to births per thousand population.

a. Births estimated by reverse projection, 1880-1934; based on registered births adjusted for underregistration, 1935-1969.

b. Stable population estimate.

c. Calculated from adjustments to 1880 stable population.

SOURCE: Ansley J. Coale and Norfleet W. Rives, Jr., "A Statistical Reconstruction of the Black Population of the United States, 1880–1970," *Population Index* 39 (1973): 26. Reprinted with permission of Population Index.

Figure 2. Crude birth rates for black and white populations, 1850–1970.

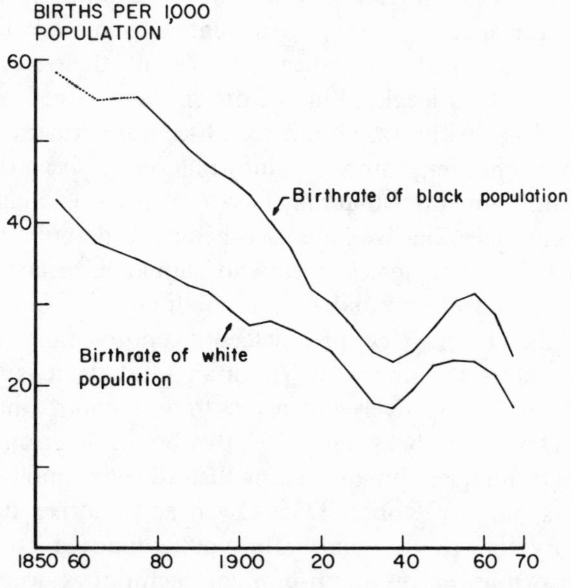

SOURCE: Ansley J. Coale and Norfleet W. Rives, Jr., "A Statistical Reconstruction of the Black Population of the United States, 1880–1970," *Population Index* 39 (1973): 26. Reprinted with permission of Population Index.

discovered that, between 1860 and 1910, black fertility was generally lower within any given region than was the fertility of their white neighbors. The one clear exception to this rule was in the South, though by 1910 even southern blacks had lower levels of childbearing than did their white neighbors. Thus, overall high levels of fertility among black Americans seem to have been associated with the fact that most black Americans lived in the South, a region in which childbearing was high among both whites and blacks.

This evidence suggests that, after 1880, both black and white Americans were responding by active choice to similar circumstances in similar ways. Since we know from various studies of black migration patterns in the early twentieth century that blacks increasingly began to take control of their own lives as they moved out of the rural south into northern urban areas, it is only reasonable to expect that at least some of these people would also seek to control their childbearing. It seems highly unlikely that men and women who were making choices about where they wanted to live would have fewer children only as entirely passive victims of ill health arising from deficient diets and widespread venereal disease.

Techniques of Family Limitation

Surprisingly, only in recent years have scholars turned their attention to the actual techniques available to nineteenth-century Americans who wished to reduce the size of their families. As historians such as Carl Degler, Linda Gordon, James Reed, and I have focused on the means by which nineteenth-century Americans might have had fewer children, important information has been discovered not only about motivations that may have been involved in using these particular techniques, but we have also helped to describe the public and private political struggles over who should have access to the means of birth control and under what conditions.

Although the current view of nineteenth-century moral standards frequently involves the image of Victorian prudery, it is clear that many Americans had relatively easy access to birth-control information if they desired it. As early as the 1830s, two books describing various birth-control techniques and advocating their use were published in the United States, one by Robert Dale Owen and another by Charles Knowlton. By the 1850s, guides for young married couples that included information on birth-control techniques were readily accessible, and advertisements appeared regularly in newspapers offering various chemicals and mechanical devices that could be used to limit births. Although federal legislation, passed in 1873 on the urging of Anthony Comstock, limited the circulation of birth-control information through the mail, advocates of family limitation quickly were able to revise their literature to overcome most of the objections of the federal legislation. Doctors rarely found any difficulty in providing information on birth-control techniques to their patients, if they desired to pass such information along. The publication of tracts advocating birth control produced rather strong responses in the nineteenth century by those who opposed widespread limitation of family size. Curiously, many of the arguments against birth control contained surprisingly detailed descriptions of a variety of techniques, so that interested parties frequently could learn as much from the opponents of birth control as they could from the advocates.

A brief listing of some of the techniques commonly recommended to nineteenth-century Americans is quite impressive. At the extremes, abstinence from sexual intercourse, if it could be done, was generally accepted, and abortion, which seems to have been widely practiced, was almost universally condemned by those involved in the debate for and against birth control. Methods relying on self-discipline that actually could provide effective means of limiting children included the following: withdrawal at critical times of intercourse; infrequent intercourse, meaning once a month or less; a rhythm method, though there was some confusion about the timing of ovulation; and intercourse without ejaculation. A number of mechanical devices also were suggested to husbands and wives who wished to limit their family size. Condoms, diaphragms, sponges to absorb semen, and a wide variety of objects that could be inserted into the woman's vagina were recommended and sold. Perhaps most awesome, however, is the long list of chemicals and botanic extracts. Some, such as ergot, cottonroot, aloes, savine, or tansy, were used to stimulate vaginal contractions that would expel either semen or a fetus. Other chemicals were to be used with water and applied with a female syringe as spermicides. The chemicals recommended ranged from the ineffective and harmless to opium, prussic acid, iodine, strychnine, lemon juice, vinegar, sulfuric acid, and, in the early twentieth century, Lysol. Undoubtedly many such chemicals had the desired spermicidal effect, but they must also have done considerable damage to the bodies of the women who used them, perhaps even making them sterile or at least uninterested in intercourse. Douching with plain water (cold was recommended by most authors) was also a common suggestion. One nineteenth-century opponent of birth control provided surprisingly detailed information about anal and oral intercourse as well as mutual masturbation, all very effective techniques for limiting births.

Not all the recommended techniques were as effective as those already mentioned. Some authors suggested a rhythm method based on a faulty understanding of the menstrual cycle. In fact, they recommended intercourse at precisely the wrong time for women whose cycles followed the normal twenty-eight-day period. The position in intercourse was believed by some to affect the chances of conception. Unless the woman was horizontal it was thought that she could not conceive. Some believed that if a woman could avoid orgasm she could also avoid pregnancy. Both of these ideas assumed that the semen had to be drawn up into the uterus by the woman's body in order for conception to occur. At least one author advocated long intervals between intercourse in the belief that the eventual union would then be so shocking to the woman's physical system that the sperm and/or egg would not survive. Vague allusions to electrical devices that render semen harmless can also be found. No comment was made, however, as to what these devices did to the women who used them. Last, but not least, violent exercise in the form of spirited dancing or riding horseback on rough roads immediately after intercourse was thought to be an effective means of preventing conception.

The fact that these techniques were included in advice manuals and were discussed with equal seriousness along with techniques that we know today to be more effective leads to several interesting conclusions. The first is that frequently discussion of birth control was based on only a limited understanding of the physical aspects of reproduction and sex. The second, however, is perhaps equally, if not more, important. In spite of the fact that many of the techniques available to nineteenth-century men and women were unpleasant if not dangerous and unreliable, they were used regularly. This suggests a rather strong motivation to have fewer children, whatever the source of that motivation may have been. A survey of the techniques recommended for limiting family size indicates that most of the means for family limitation that are available to twentieth-century Americans were also available in the previous century. The only significant technological breakthrough in birth control has been the development since 1960 of the oral contraceptive pill. Thus, reduced childbearing resulted from decisions to have fewer children, whatever the effort, but not from technological breakthroughs that made such action feasible for the first time.

Because many of the nineteenth-century techniques placed control of family size, at least to a limited degree, in the hands of wives, explanations based solely on motives of males for reduced family size must be considered inadequate. The need to emphasize women's involvement in the decision to limit births is obvious to anyone who reads this literature. Over and over the manuals mention that women who sought advice on birth control did so in order to improve their lives. Some feared additional pregnancies for reasons of personal health; others wanted to devote more time to their families or to other interests; all sought to bring some sensible order and dignity into their lives. It is difficult to determine how widespread these motives were, because most of the men who wrote the literature on birth control were not overly sympathetic to women's efforts to better themselves, except where a woman's husband was behaving in an extremely cruel fashion. Edward Foote's advocacy of the cervical diaphragm in 1864 because it, "places conception entirely under the control of the wife, to whom it actually belongs," is a rare early instance of male support for women controlling reproduction for their own reasons.

The participants in the debate on birth control did not ignore male reasons for desiring to limit the size of their family. Some advocated limitations to sexual activity solely on the grounds of insuring the health of husbands and their wives in order that they would be better able to provide adequate physical and economic care for the children that they did have. Sometimes birth control was recommended as a means of improving the future chances of children by allowing the concentration of family resources on one or two sons or daughters. In other cases, the immediate avoidance of poverty was the source of the recommendation for limiting family size. In the end, what is clear is that nineteenth-century Americans understood both the overall importance of motivation in the practice of birth control and that the needs and interests of both husband and wife were involved in the decisions of a particular couple regarding whether or not to have an additional child.

Some interesting and important insights on the political aspect of fertility control have emerged from the recent studies on nineteenth-century techniques of family limitation. For example, James Mohr's work shows how public efforts to restrict abortion in the nineteenth century often involved contests between male physicians and female midwives over who would supervise pregnancy and childbirth, and control the fees associated with such service. Initial legislation restricting abortion defined as criminal only those who produced abortions. Women who sought abortions or bought chemicals that were understood to produce abortions were exempt from any kind of criminal condemnation. Nineteenth-century legislators were apparently unwilling to penalize women who used abortion until only lower-class wives and daughters relied heavily on this technique to limit the number of births they might have. Interestingly, the long-term patterns in fertility control described in the statistical studies we examined earlier suggest that the adoption of legislation restricting abortion, and other laws such as those advocated by Comstock making it illegal to circulate any kind of advice regarding birth control, seem to have had limited effect on long-term fertility trends. The overall decline in fertility appears to have continued at approximately the same rate despite the debate regarding the wisdom of such control and legislation limiting access to certain means of family limitation. Curiously, public discussion of birth control reappeared on a widespread and acceptable basis only as the decline in childbearing temporarily came to an end in the mid-1930s.

On the private, domestic level political discussions involving the relative distribution of power within the family raised questions regarding women's rights to control their own bodies and therefore to control their own futures as persons who were more than mothers, and the common expectation that wives should sacrifice their own particular self-interests to the needs of the family. In the nineteenth century, efforts by women to free themselves from the necessity of bearing children in order to pursue other intersts were both approved and condemned in strong and emotional language. Unfortunately, it is not known whether the same level of emotion existed within individual families as decisions were made to limit births. Few nineteenth-century men or women ever recorded how or why they decided to have or not to have children. Perhaps such decisions were simply too personal to commit to paper, or perhaps the process was never sufficiently clear in an individual family to be full conscious decision. It is entirely possible that smaller families were the result of many minor decisions or arguments about whether or not to have a child at any particular moment, so that a couple never did sit down and decide what their ultimate family size would be ten years hence. It is possible that the long-term decline in childbearing should be seen as the gradual accumulation of a number of small decisions that grew into a major change rather than the result of one major decision occurring within a particular family and ultimately in groups of families.

Birth Control—A Different Meaning

One final aspect of nineteenth-century birth control deserves mention here, although in this case what is meant by birth control differs considerably from the way in which the term has been used so far. Birth control most commonly refers to efforts to limit childbearing. Another possible meaning, however, includes efforts that emerged during the nineteenth century to manage childbirth. A recent study of the cultural context of childbirth in nineteenth and early twentieth-century America by Richard and Dorothy Wertz has emphasized that birth is more than a biological phenomenon, involving both cultural and sociological factors. In particular, the Wertzes have demonstrated that childbirth has changed dramatically since the early nineteenth century in five significant ways. In the eighteenth century, American women gave birth at home, surrounded and helped by family and female friends. Today most women deliver their children under the control of male doctors, who frequently view childbirth as a medical problem. Over time, a woman's attendants have come to intervene more and more in what was once considered a natural process that was allowed to run its course. This increased interference has been partly explained by the need for both doctors and their patients to justify the cost of having a physician in attendance at the birth of a child instead of a midwife, and partly by efforts, growing out of a desire for a longer life, to control as much of the biological side of being human as possible. An important result of this change is the shift in attitudes about the body. In order to facilitate intervention by physicians, and to overcome nineteenth-century inhibitions about having men touch women in very personal ways, women gradually came to see themselves as having a body that could be manipulated instead of being a body in which control automatically extended to emotional and spiritual states. The shift in who attended the woman at time of delivery, from midwife to doctor, preceded the eventual decision by most women to leave their homes at time of delivery to go into hospitals. Recently, significant reductions in infant and maternal mortality at time of birth, combined with feminist critiques regarding how male doctors treat female patients, has produced a significant movement by a number of women to remain in their home at time of birth.

What is Known

In summarizing what is known about the nineteenth-century decline in fertility the following points stand out. First, the decline itself was significant. After 1900, childbearing was probably no more than fifty percent of what it had been in 1800 (see Table IV). In addition, the patterns of childbearing during the nineteenth century had been complex, varying significantly by region, occupation, income, ethnic group, and time. However, eventually almost all Americans participated in the limitation of family size, although some did not do so in any significant way until after the start of the twentieth century. Motivations, in retrospect, are clearly complex and involve not only broad changes in social and economic structures but also shifts in values that determined how persons might choose to respond to particular social and economic pressures. A fundamental aspect of motivation was whether a man or woman, faced with an unfamiliar problem, believed a response such as limiting family size was possible and appropriate. By the middle of the nineteenth century a number of Americans were aware of the revolution in childbearing. They were less certain, however, of whether this change was desirable, whether it should actually be encouraged, or whether it was a change for the worse.

One final point deserves mention. Explanations for fertility control in the nineteenth century frequently assume that patterns of childbearing and motives regarding whether or not to have an additional child were the same after 1950 as they were before 1900. This is not, however, self-evident. The behavior and attitudes of nineteenth-century couples may have been substantially different from the men and women of today. In the nineteenth century, Americans began to choose not to have children. Today, most couples assume it is possible not to have children and so ultimately choose to have them. In addition, sex and reproduction have become increasingly separated, particularly since 1960 with the widespread dissemination of oral contraceptives. This separation clearly was not possible in nineteenth-century America. Future studies of the fertility decline in the nineteenth century will no doubt continue to explore the motives that produced this shift, but any such explorations must be conscious of the question of whether or not the reasons twentieth-century Americans limit their families are the same as those that encouraged their nineteenth-century ancestors to embark on one of the most fundamental revolutions in human history.

Chapter 3

Matters of Life and Death

Interest in the Subject

In his introduction to a recent interdisciplinary collection of essays on the cultural context of death in America, David Stannard observed, "Of all the profound concerns and fears of men in any age, death is one of the few constants; it may be the only one." Sex may rival death in terms of inherent human interest but certainly there are few other aspects of life that match these two areas of concern. The meaning and imminence of death have fascinated humans since before written records, as evidence from burial mounds and early paintings testify. Thus, an interest in the patterns of death, the paths to health, and the psychological aspects of mortality in the past is not surprising.

There are, however, other sources of interest in the study of mortality in the past. In the eighteenth century, efforts to provide insurance for the widows of Protestant clergymen in New England and the Middle Colonies led to the collection of information on mortality patterns in those regions. At the end of the nineteenth century and in the early twentieth century life insurance companies devoted some attention to the collection of historical records on patterns of death in order to supplement the sketchy records available for contemporary populations. In fact, many early demographers in the United States were employed by life insurance companies.

At the end of the nineteenth century, as the medical profession began to be more firmly established and gain respect within American society, medical history began to emerge as a subject of some interest. Often early students of medical history were doctors who were interested in studying the past of their own profession as a means of relaxation. These doctors, and the first scholars who studied medical history professionally, frequently directed their attentions toward doctors who made significant or colorful contributions, technological discoveries, quaint practices, or the emergence of professionally important organizations such as the American Medical Association or local or regional boards of health. Early medical historians were often concerned with tracing the progress of American doctors in their efforts to eliminate alternative forms of medical practice, which had been available to the American population in the mid-nineteenth century.

Recently, medical history has broadened its interest to include the consumers as well as the vendors of medical care, and the social history of medicine. The medical problems of a community when confronted by an epidemic or mundane matters, such as how a town attempts to clean its streets and get rid of its garbage, have been recognized as part of medical, or perhaps more appropriately, health history. The growth of newspapers and magazines in the nineteenth century, and the emergence of radio and television as mass media in the twentieth century, have been linked in interesting ways to the widespread circulation of patent medicines and quack medical devices.

Assumptions involved in the demographic transition theory have also served to direct our attention to patterns of mortality in the past. In the classical exposition of the theory, the death rate was assumed to fall before any changes in fertility were apparent. The assumption was that improved economic conditions generally produced improved social well-being from better diet, housing, clothing, or other factors that increased income could buy. In situations where it has not always been possible to measure the standard of living directly, some scholars have turned to the study of patterns of health and death in order to determine whether different groups have experienced improvements in social and economic well-being at different moments in the past.

Finally, a series of current political and social problems have led scholars to study a variety of issues in the past, all of which either directly or indirectly bear on levels of life expectancy. A concern for the environment has produced interest in the location and spread of disease, in the relationship between human activity, land, and disease, and in past levels of various forms of pollution. In addition, students have recently begun to explore the extent of alcoholism and drug addiction in nineteenth-century America. Marked increases in the twentieth century of the proportion of the population over the age of sixty-five have encouraged an examination of the role of older people in earlier periods of American history. It is not surprising that an interest in the aged in society also involves some concerns with patterns of illness and mortality. Finally, concerns with sexism and racism in American society have led to studies of how doctors treated or mistreated subordinate groups in American society such as women, blacks, or Indians. It is evident from this work that not all Americans received equally effective or equally beneficial medical care.

Records

Studying mortality in the past is often a difficult task. Records may be incomplete and are often subject to widely varying interpretations because early observers had different scientific and subjective perspectives than do twentieth-century scholars. Even if earlier records are to be believed, and they are sometimes subject to serious biases, the testimony that they include is not always easy to translate into current terms.

Consider for a moment the records that doctors left regarding particular diseases which were common in earlier centuries. Recall that the ability to identify specific causes for specific diseases is only about a hundred years old. Doctors working before that time frequently thought about diseases in terms of readily observable symptoms rather than specific causes or internal disorders. This leads to a series of particularly perplexing problems. For example, doctors frequently linked different diseases with common symptoms, or they described as separate diseases the several distinct stages of one particular malady because of the different types of suffering that the victim displayed. In addition, descriptions in twentieth-century textbooks based on laboratory or hospital observations of diseases may not have much resemblance to the kind of symptoms which would have been observed in a seventeenth-century community. Twentieth-century physicans rarely see some of the maladies which were major killers in the seventeenth or eighteenth centuries, and certainly they rarely see them in a completely untreated form. Furthermore, differences in treatment from one century to another may have an effect on the symptoms that patients manifest. It is probable that the practice of bleeding produced different responses in a patient than would treatment with penicillin. Finally, it is entirely possible that particular diseases either mutate or become adapted to the population in which they are located, and so the symptoms of one period are not the same as those observed at a later date. Since medical practice frequently involves certain philosophical assumptions about the cause of the disease, it may well be that doctors in the past simply would not have noted particular symptoms, considering them unimportant, whereas a twentieth-century physician would regard that particualr symptom as indicative of the presence of a particular disease. In spite of these difficulties, we do know a surprising amount not only about the causes of death in the past but also about the overall levels of life expectancy. Nonetheless, it is important to treat any statements about health conditions in early America with a certain degree of caution.

Ultimately, most studies about the actual level of mortality in previous centuries rely on various kinds of lists of deaths. Among the earliest available records are those kept by churches or communities in which an individual's name would be entered into a book when he or she died, along with some indication of age and possible cause of death (see Table III, page 20). These early vital statistics records are not always complete or accurate and frequently cover only a very small part of the population. By the 1930s, however, these early parish and community records evolved into an extensive death registration system run by the United States government covering at least ninety percent of the American population. Other lists of deaths include what were known in the eighteenth century as bills of mortality. These were frequently constructed by interested scholars from the parish registers and were simply summary tables of the various individual entries noting how many people of particular ages had died, aggregating deaths under various broad causes, and sometimes indicating what times of year mortality seems to have been most common. In the nineteenth century, similar kinds of information were sometimes presented in federal or states censuses or in the sanitary reports produced for the improvement of health conditions in certain communities. Lists of deaths by themselves offer some information on mortality but frequently are not very helpful unless additional data is available on the size and composition of the population.

Since particular diseases do not strike all ages, sexes, or races with equal intensity, the accuracy of any study of mortality depends, at least in part, on the student's ability to determine who exactly is exposed to the greatest risk of dying in any particular period. Such information makes it possible to distinguish between changes caused by improvement or deterioration of health, and shifts resulting from more or fewer people who are especially vulnerable to diseases common in a particular time and place. If information on the size and composition of the population is available from censuses or other similar sources, it can be used along with the lists of deaths to calculate such measures as life expectancy, the probability of survival from one age to some more advanced age, the number of individuals dying in any particular year out of every 1,000 people in the population, and the average age at death. In the absence of lists of deaths, information on the growth or decline of the population can indicate approximate levels of mortality, although it is obvious that using this kind of information depends on some knowledge of the levels of childbearing and migration.

In situations where scholars have not had the ideal sources available to them, or where they have been interested as much in attitudes about mortality as in the actual level at which people died, scholars have been able to use other sources in imaginative and inventive ways. Among the more interesting sources are wills, literature and art, legislation and reports of various sanitary commissions, which frequently reflect the political struggles revolving around efforts to improve health, and the extent of orphanage in a particular society. Records evolving from burial practices have been particularly informative whether they emerge from descriptions of funeral customs, explorations of the carvings on gravestones, an interest in the geographic location of cemetaries, or the actual study of skeletal remains. The necessity of an interdisciplinary approach to this material should be obvious since the skills involved in interpreting skeletal remains are not those that can be used to interpret the meaning of art or gravestone carvings. Furthermore, neither of these skills are particualrly useful when it comes to interpreting evidence from legal documents such as wills.

Some Current Issues

The issues and interests that have attracted various scholars to the study of the history of mortality in America from Columbus to the present defy easy summary or ready periodization. In order to provide some detail about some of the actual concerns of students of mortality in the past, and to show the interdisciplinary perspectives involved, seven of the more important topics have been selected for discussion here. These topics include several that are concerned with the actual levels and patterns of mortality and others involving some of the psychological and social aspects of health and death. In the discussion that follows we will look first at questions involving the size and decline of the Indian populations in early America, at patterns of mortality in early seventeenth-century Virginia, at health conditions among black slaves in the American South, and at recent efforts to explain the dramatic improvements in life expectancy which Americans have experienced since 1880. Discussion will then turn to the examination of the meaning of disease in society and how definitions of disease have changed over time. Then, a study of doctors and their relationships to their peers, patients, and society will be undertaken. Finally, there will be an exploration of the changing views of the meaning of death, and how individuals and their families, friends, and society were expected to respond in different periods of American history.

1. Indian Mortality

The size of the Indian population in the Americas in the years just before Columbus established permanent contact between the Americas and Europe, Africa, and Asia is a subject of considerable debate. This is an issue which is of interest because it not only affects our interpretations of early American history, but also sheds light on the possible catastrophic consequences of exposing populations to unfamiliar disease.

Estimates of scholars who have studied the problem of how many people were living in the Americas before 1492 have ranged from a population of 8 million to over 110 million people, obviously a range of considerable disagreement. Since there is general agreement that the total Indian population was about 4 million people in 1650, serious questions are raised as a result of the various estimates of the size of the population prior to Columbus's arrival. The lowest totals suggest a level of demographic catastrophe equal to, or perhaps slightly greater than, that experienced in Europe during the bubonic plague epidemics of the mid-fourteenth century, and the higher estimates of population suggest a catastrophe that is almost beyond imagination.

These are questions of some concern. At issue is an understanding of the size and complexity of early Indian societies. In addition, answers to these questions may tell us about the potential of the New World environment to support human life in the absence of highly refined agricultural technology. Answers to these questions are also important if scholars are to understand the extent of dislocation produced by the arrival of Europeans in the Americas, regardless of whether this dislocation was produced intentionally as a result of war against the Indians and efforts to extract work from them, or accidentally via the introduction of new and unfamiliar diseases. Moral issues regarding the interpretation of early American history are raised depending on whether one sees Europeans arriving in a virgin or widowed land, whether they are colonizing or conquering, or whether they were pioneering into a wilderness or resettling territory taken from already established civilizations. On reflection, it may be argued that the difference in morality between a demographic catastrophe in which a third to a half of the population disappears as opposed to one where ninety-five percent of the population disappears is not too great. Nonetheless, the debate on the size of the Indian population has involved some moral concern.

Initially, the debate has been one involving skills of literary criticism as much as knowledge of demographic techniques. This reflects in part the nature of the sources on the early Indian population and in part the interests of the scholars involved. Those who favor low estimates of the Indian population argue that there is, in fact, no hard evidence of large populations. In the absence of censuses or unequivocal archeological records of large populations, such scholars argue that European observers who suggest large Indian populations are by and large unreliable. Christopher Columbus, for example, frequently made observations about America which indicated that he did not understand what, in fact, he had discovered. In light of these observations, scholars raise the question about whether his estimates about American population totals should be given any more credit than any of his other comments. A second source of information on the early American population was the Spanish monk Bartolome de Las Casas, an admitted polemicist who was arguing in favor of limiting Spanish exploitations of Indian labor and for the importation of Africans to provide the needed work force for Spanish exploitation of the New World. On a more general level of criticism, scholars have observed that individuals of the fifteenth and sixteenth centuries frequently had very weak quantitative skills and used numbers very loosely. In addition, they frequently wished to boast about their importance in the conquest of America and hence would be inclined to emphasize large populations in order to make their own exploits seem all the more impressive.

Although there is merit in many of these observations, there are some assumptions which proponents of small population sizes make which need to be examined. On the one hand, they frequently have a perspective of history in which the past is always inferior to the present, and the present will lead to an ever-better future. Thus, it is almost necessary for them to find the past as having smaller populations and, by implication, though not always explicitly stated, more primitive societies. Any evidence of large, complex, and sophisticated societies would be very disruptive to this point of view. Occasionally such scholars have arbitrarily reduced the estimates not only of sixteenth-century observers but also of contemporary ethnographers who have collected a vast amount of information. They seem to offer no particular explanation for these reductions other than their belief that past populations simply could not have been very large.

The upward revision in estimates of how many Americans there were prior to Columbus's arrival is a fairly recent trend and has proceeded along several lines of study. Scholars who have reexamined the texts, which earlier students of the question found so unreliable, have argued that, indeed, these sources are remarkably consistent and have raised the question about why early observers should be expected to lie. Their answers have been quite different from the earlier scholars in that they have felt the early comments to be reasonably reliable. In addition, they point out with some merit that the earliest comments on the size of the American population often were recorded after a minimum of twenty years of contact between European and American populations, so there had been ample time for American Indians to have been subjected to the ravages of Old World diseases. Thus, from the revisionist perspective, it is necessary to project larger populations back from these early observations to the period just before contact was established.

A second impetus for upward revisions of estimates of the early American population has been the recent establishment of the mechanism by which such a demographic catastrophe could have occurred. In the nineteenth and twentieth centuries populations have been observed which have been exposed to new and unfamiliar diseases with resulting mortality in the neighborhood of fifty to ninety-five percent. On the assumption that the same kind of catastrophe was possible in the sixteenth century, some scholars have been willing to project backward from the low point around 1650 to much larger earlier populations. It is evident from contemporary texts that the first Americans were exposed in a relatively short period of time to a shocking number of unfamiliar and highly contagious and fatal diseases from the Old World. Major killers that were introduced into the Americas with the arrival of Columbus and his successors included smallpox, measles, whooping cough, chicken pox, bubonic plague, typhus, malaria, diphtheria, amoebic dysentery, influenza, and a variety of worms. It is possible, though not certain, that yellow fever also arrived with the Spanish explorers. Such an onslaught of diseases is almost unprecedented in human history and is certainly possible of producing the kind of demographic catastrophe that scholars argue must have happened. Although there is still widespread disagreement about how great the catastrophe was, there is an emerging consensus that the four million surviving Indians alive in the Americas around 1650 probably came from populations which, in the years just before Columbus, counted between 50 and 100 million individuals.

Although backward projections of the Indian population based on assumed analogies between their experience and the experience of small populations in the nineteenth and twentieth centuries are convincing, there are other materials which have lent support to the conclusion that the early Indian populations must have been quite sizeable. For example, new texts have been discovered involving early levels of tribute expected by the Spanish from the Indians. These texts, although not directly including statements on population size, make it clear that only fairly large numbers of Indians could have produced the amount of wealth that the Spanish expected to extract from the native Americans. In addition, recent archeological discoveries involving both aerial photography and work on the ground have shown evidence of sizeable agricultural communities involving sophisticated agricultural techniques even in relatively hostile environments. The implications of these archeological remains are first, that the American environment was capable of sustaining a fairly sizeable population, and, second, that such a population must have been present in order to both require and produce the kind of agricultural structures that have been discovered.

Studies of the various types of blood in early American populations have demonstrated clear physical differences between New and Old World inhabitants. This lends credence to the argument that Indians in the Americas had been isolated from Asia for a long period of time so that immunities to the diseases that were brought by the Europeans would not have been present. In addition, there is growing ethnographic evidence of rapid shifts in both the location and life styles of the various Indian tribes that lived on the North American plains. This evidence suggests dramatic population declines, in most cases with ensuing cultural alterations. In fairness, however, it should be noted that at least some of these shifts may hae been produced not by the introduction of diseases but by changes in climate occurring some years before Columbus's arrival and disrupting agricultrual practices in the central and upper Mississippi River Valley and on the northen plains.

2. Mortality in Early Virginia

Early American historians have long been interested in how rapidly and how completely European society was recreated in the American environment. As scholars have begun to explore questions revolving around American families and how they related to this more general issue, it is not surprising that they have begun to explore levels of mortality in the early colonies. Initially, students of the demographic history of the future United States focused on New England where they discovered that the Puritans, if they survived to adulthood, frequently could expect to live a remarkably long time, at least within the context of the seventeenth and eighteenth centuries.

However, in recent years, the focus broadened to include the Chesapeake colonies of Virginia and Maryland where the settlers appear to have faced a much more dangerous environment. In fact, the population may not have been capable of replacing itself in the Chesapeake until somewhere around 1700, almost a century after Jamestown was founded. Part of the explanation for the inability of the early Chesapeake population to grow without substantial immigration can be related to low levels of childbearing and an extraordinary imbalance of the sex ratio in which men outnumbered women by approximately six to one. But it is also clear that mortality was exceptionally high, especially in the early years of settlement. Between 1618 and 1624, about six thousand individuals moved to Virginia to join the four hundred English men and women already in residence. It is shocking today, just as it was to the English government in 1624, to discover that at the end of this period of migration the Virginia population included fewer than thirteen hundred individuals. An Indian attack on the encroaching English in 1622 accounted for fewer than three hundred of the deaths.

Recent efforts to study the causes and consequences of the relatively high mortality of the Chesapeake have drawn on the skills and techniques of a number of different disciplines and used data in imaginative ways.

One explanation for the high levels of mortality in early Virginia is essentially cultural. Edmund Morgan has suggested that Virginians died at extraordinary rates in the early years of settlement primarily because they failed to alter patterns of behavior that they brought with them from England. Morgan argues, with some reason, that in the late sixteenth and early seventeenth centuries England suffered from relative overpopulation. Large numbers of English men and women were underemployed and, as a result, not only developed habits of working a minimal number of hours but also came to expect low levels of diet and nutrition. Ill health and high levels of mortality were common phenomena in the England that sent colonists to the New World. As a result, according to Morgan, the early settlers of Virginia did not find it surprising when high levels of mortality occurred in the colony. Nor did they take advantage of relatively large amounts of available land to improve their diet. They were so conditioned to working a minimal number of hours that they refused to work longer hours in order to provide themselves with more food. One of the major problems the Virginia Company faced in its early years was not only supplying sufficient laborers to the Jamestown colony but also getting them to work sufficient hours to support themselves. The implication is that early Virginians need not have succumbed as rapidly as they did in the New World if only they had been willing to give up patterns of behavior suited to life in England and adapt themselves to the new environment in a more efficient and practical fashion. The fact that Morgan emphasizes labor, or rather the lack thereof, is not surprising considering his main concern is to explain why the Virginia colony ultimately came to depend heavily on black slaves rather than white servants or free men.

Morgan's explanation has not gone unchallenged, however. Karen Kupperman has argued that the apparent apathy and lethargy visible among the early Virginia settlers was caused not so much by English culture but by a situation that is very similar to that experienced by people put into twentieth-century prison camps. Kupperman claims that the primary cause of death in the colony was a combination of malnutrition and a loss of psychological resistance brought about by fear, anxiety, and a lack of leadership. Studies of prisoners of war during World War II and the Korean War demonstrate that individuals who had very limited diets began to exhibit forms of behavior that could easily be interpreted as apathy and lethargy. When combined with prison situations in which leaders were missing from the prison camp, individuals frequently appeared to give up their struggle for life and often seemed to welcome death. In certain circumstances, even when diet was sufficient, a lack of leadership apparently made prisoners willing to accept death rather than continue to struggle under highly adverse circumstances to maintain an unpleasant life for an indeterminant future amount of time.

The comparison with Virginia is obvious. The early settlers were isolated in a strange and unfamiliar environment, were poorly fed, and suffered from a lack of leadership in some years and highly whimsical and arbitrary exercises of authority in others. Under such conditions, Kupperman argues, individuals found themselves in highly stressful situations where, given the lack of a balanced diet in Virginia, it was only natural that some of them either became apathetic, or exhibited signs of behavior that could be interpreted as apathetic, and so succumbed to the ravages of various diseases in Virginia at extraordinarily rapid rates. This explanation is particularly interesting because it combines both physiological and psychological dimensions in attempting to understand why the early Virginians died with extraordinary rapidity.

Other studies of the situation in early Virginia have depended more on strictly biological explanations. One of these, done by Carville Earle, a geographer, looks at the actual site of the Jamestown settlement and how the residential patterns of the Virginians evolved over time. Assuming that the climate and geography of the Chesapeake Bay region have not changed dramatically since the seventeenth century, Earle has demonstrated that the choice of Jamestown for the initial settlement in Virginia was unfortunate. He argues that Jamestown was located on a point in the James River where seasonal variations in the flow of fresh water down the river into the saltwater areas of the bay made health conditions particularly hazardous, especially in the late summer. In the early spring, water flowing down the James River is of sufficient volume to wash any wastes which the Jamestown settlers would have deposited into the waters out into Chesapeake Bay. In addition, the heavy flow of fresh water would have meant that drinking water would have been reasonably safe at this time of year. However, as spring gave way to summer, and the flow of the river subsided considerably, saltwater from the Chesapeake would move up the James River, actually passing the settlement at Jamestown.

This had two rather serious effects on residents of the community. First, waste materials that had been washed out into the bay no longer were cleared from the drinking water and so the Jamestown inhabitants began to consume their own wastes with expected ill effects. The second problem came from the fact that they began to drink saltwater, which also has ill effects on the human system. Earle makes use of his geographer's expertise to point out that as the saltwater began to invade the upper reaches of the James River in late summer the rotational forces of the earth would produce more dense concentrations of wastes and saltwater on the Jamestown side of the river rather than on the southern bank.

Earle argues that some of the early Virginia leaders recognized the unfortunate situation of the town and made efforts to disperse the English settlers to sites that were more conducive to good health, even though they might not be as easily defended against Indians. His reading of the evidence convinces him that during the periods when the early Virginians were scattered around, generally above the line in the rivers where saltwater penetrated and near fresh water springs, the colony did surprisingly well. At other times, when external forces or leadership decisions reconcentrated many of the Virginia settlers in these dangerous environments, high levels of mortality once again appeared.

Interestingly, these same ebbs and flows of leadership which scattered and reconcentrated the colonists closely parallel Kupperman's periods of dynamic and ineffective leadership which encouraged or reduced apathy among the settlers. Thus, Earle provides a fairly simple biological and geographical explanation for a phenomenon that Kupperman sees as analogous to twentieth-century prisoner-of-war camp experiences. Earle certainly would not deny the importance of malnutrition in producing high levels of mortality in early Virginia, but he does emphasize the contribution of amoebic dysentery, typhoid, and saltwater poisoning, which could be traced directly to the location of where Virginians lived.

These studies are interesting as explanations for why mortality was high in Virginia in the early years of settlement, but they ultimately do not explain why the Virginia population had trouble sustaining itself until the start of the eighteenth century, for long before then Virginians had moved well beyond the areas of saltwater invasion in the summer and had overcome initial problems of leadership. Darrett and Anita Rutman have argued persuasively that malaria was one of the principal causes of high levels of mortality in the Chesapeake throughout the seventeenth century, and have made a convincing case that the presence of this particular disease goes a long way to explaining the differences between life expectancy in the Chesapeake and in New England. They, too, have observed that early Virginians frequently showed evidence of lethargy and low productivity. However, they feel the cause was endemic malaria; malnutrition certainly was present, but the contribution of English culture or a situation similar to World War II prisoner-of-war camps may not be necessry to explain what is quite possibly a simple biological phenomenon.

The Rutman study is of special interest to us because it demonstrates the extraordinary variety of materials that historians must call upon in order to understand the levels of mortality in early Virginia. In an extremely interesting discussion of the nature of malaria, they describe not only the complex cycle of malaria involving both human beings and mosquitoes as hosts for the malaria parasite but also a series of different types of malaria to which Virginians may have been subject. This is particularly important because certain forms of malaria are extremely lethal. Others merely deplete energy without endangering life. The patterns of malarial infection are made more complicated by the fact that different types of mosquitoes infect human populations with different malarial strains. This requires some knowledge of the habits of these little pests since mosquitoes vary considerably in the kind of water that they prefer to breed in, some doing better in saltwater and some doing better in fresh water. In addition, mosquitoes apparently vary considerably in the time of day that they prefer to bite human beings. Some prefer to feast at night while others are around and about during the daylight. The interactions of various malarial parasites with different breeding and biting patterns of the mosquito hosts meant that early Virginians were subject to widely varied dangers of malaria depending on where they lived.

This conclusion is obviously very close to Earle's emphasis on the different dangers of various communities in Virginia. It also suggests that it should not be surprising to discover that Virginians who lived relatively close together were nonetheless exposed to dramatically different conditions of health and death. A few miles could make the difference in the type of mosquito and hence the type of malaria that might strike an individual, and in whether or not wastes deposited in the river would be washed into Chesapeake Bay all year round or only part of the year.

It is important to keep in mind that none of these studies is interested in mortality levels in early Virginia solely from the demographic point of view. All of these works either implicitly or explicitly contrast Virginians' experience to that of the New England colonists, either in terms of environment or social organization. In addition, they are all interested in the consequences of high mortality in early Virginia. Morgan was concerned with the evolution of the labor system in early Virignia. Kupperman and Earle were intrigued with the kind of leadership that the early Virginia colony received, with Earle emphasizing the remarkable environmental sophistication that at least several early Virignia leaders seemed to have. Finally, the Rutmans moved from their rather convincing demonstration that malaria was present in Virginia in the seventeenth century to speculate on what this meant in terms of family stability, community strength, and the economic productivity of the early settlers. In general, they contended that in contrast to New England, Virginia was probably a place where human life was less secure, human relationships were more unpredictable, and economic productivity was both lower and more exploitive because of the uncertainty of life. Thus, early American society quickly evolved two quite distinct traditions that have been influential throughout our history. One was oriented toward stability, community, and the family; the other encouraged exploitation and carelessness, eventually giving rise to a major commitment to human slavery. At least part of this difference can be traced to fundamental realities of life and death that distinguished New England from the Chesapeake.

3. The Health of Slaves

The health and mortality conditions of black Americans under slavery is a subject that has also received recent attention from historians and other scholars. Efforts to assess the mortality experience of black Americans generally have two somewhat overlapping origins. One is an interest in the effects of slavery on the victims—was slavery a harsh system or was it ultimately, if not beneficial, at least not overly detrimental to the enslaved blacks? A second line of inquiry raises the question about whether black Americans have had a history that is essentially the same or different from their white counterparts. If it is different, in what way is it different and why?

The studies of mortality among the early white settlers of Virginia have made us aware of the importance of geography on a local scale. Philip Curtin, a student of the slave trade from the sixteenth through the nineteenth centuries, has contributed to our understanding not only of black mortality in the New World but also to our need to be aware of geographical effects on disease and mortality on a much wider scale. Curtin observed that even though the number of Africans imported into North America comprised only a very small proportion of the total number of slaves brought into the New World, the Afro-American population in the United States in the twentieth century has increased dramatically from what it had been in the eighteenth century, especially when compared to blacks living in the Caribbean or Brazil, regions which received the overwhelming majority of slaves at the height of the slave trade.

One possible explanation for the extraordinary growth of the black population in North America is simply that slaves there were treated better than those in either the Caribbean or Brazil. This may be true. On the other hand, Curtin has also argued that part of the explanation may be traceable to distinctly different disease environments. In the Caribbean, for example, dense settlements of Europeans and Africans, and in some areas Indians as well, existed in a climate conducive to diseases thriving on a year-round basis; in such places life expectancy was extraordinarily low. In contrast, North America was a relatively favorable place, partly because settlements were not as dense and hence a form of natural quarantine may have been in effect to slow down the spread of diseases, and partly because the seasons are more pronounced as one moves farther north along the American coast, which means that during certain times of the year diseases such as malaria or dysentery are less violent or are altogether absent. Therefore, killers that may have been endemic in the Caribbean might appear farther north only irregularly as epidemics.

In his study of the contribution of blacks in the evolution of early South Carolina society, Peter Wood has emphasized the role of Africans in establishing rice as the basis of the South Carolina economy. Wood describes how blacks were tremendously important in the development of rice as the cash crop of South Carolina not only because they brought a knowledge of how rice was grown from their West African homelands, but also because they had a capacity to survive in the low coastal regions of South Carolina where rice was grown. Because rice thrives best in low swampy regions conducive to breeding mosquito populations, malaria was a common danger in South Carolina in the seventeenth and eighteenth centuries. At the time, many observers commented on the remarkable capacity for blacks to survive malaria, apparently much more effectively than whites.

Wood makes use of biological and medical data to demonstrate why this should be so. All human populations are subject to occasional mutations of the genes which produce twisted red blood cells knows as sickle cells. In general, this sickle cell trait is bad for individuals because such deformed blood cells do not carry oxygen as effectively as normal red blood cells. However, sickle cells also make it less possible for malaria parasites to take hold in the human body. Thus, individuals who developed their sickle cell trait in a malarial environment find that their blood's reduced capacity to carry oxygen is more than offset by an increased capacity to fight the ravages of malarial infections. As a result, the sickle cell trait can frequently be found in parts of the world where malaria is common, whether that is in West Africa or in parts of the Mediterranean basin. The important point to note here is that slaves imported from West Africa frequently did have the sickle cell trait and so were better able to survive malarial dangers in South Carolina, and obviously in the Chesapeake as well. The English had not been exposed extensively to malaria and so had not developed this particular blood characteristic which provided significant defenses against the infections of malaria.

In spite of this relative advantage in malarial areas, black Americans probably had levels of life expectancy lower than their white contemporaries. This was partly the result of being worked long hours in environments that not only bred malarial mosquitoes but other dangers as well, and, in addition, as slaves moved out of malarial regions into territories where other crops were grown, the sickle cell trait would cease to be an advantage and would become a detriment to their health.

In general, most studies of slavery in American society focus not on the colonial period but on the fifty years preceding the Civil War. Therefore, it is interesting to expand our perspective to include the mortality conditions facing black Americans in the half century prior to emancipation. Recently, Robert Fogel and Stanley Engerman concluded that slave owners took care of their human property and gave their slaves adequate medical attention and food if only to protect the financial investment that they had in their slaves. Among other things, they examined the diet of slaves, which generally consisted of pork, cornmeal, and molasses, with the addition of some green vegetables during the summer, and argued that on the basis of calories, and to some extent nutrition, black Americans generally ate as well as their northern free white counterparts. This incidentally may say more about the low standard of living among both white and black workers in America in the first half of the nineteenth century than it does about the good life of the slave. Nonetheless, the implication is that the standard of living for slaves was more than adequate to sustain them in relative good health. It is somewhat surprising then to discover that most of the limited demographic data on slave mortality seems to indicate that life expectancy among black Americans in the first half of the nineteenth century was anywhere from five to ten years lower than that of white Americans.

Perhaps the presence of the sickle cell trait might explain part of this difference, but at least two recent studies suggest that blacks were worse off in terms of mortality and health than whites, at least in part because of diet. In one fascinating exploration, Richard Steckel makes use of lists kept by ship captains involved in carrying slaves from the Chesapeake to the Gulf Coast for sale in Mississippi, Alabama, and Louisiana in which the heights and ages of the slaves were recorded. This study examines patterns of growth to show not only how tall the slaves ultimately grew to be but also when spurts of growth occurred. Assuming that the twentieth century pattern of the adolescent growth spurt, in which diet and the amount of body fat determine both when and how long rapid growth will occur, was much the same in the nineteenth century, the heights of the younger slaves suggest that black Americans in the early nineteenth century had significantly lower levels of nutrition than do contemporary Americans. In addition, similar information on white populations in the North in the ealry nineteenth century, and for some Europeans in the nineteenth century as well, indicate that nutritional levels among slaves were in fact lower than those of northern whites, but were somewhat better than those of nineteenth-century Europeans.

The conclusion that blacks suffered from a degree of malnutrition is reenforced when the specific elements that went into the common diet on southern plantations are examined, especially in the context of particular needs that blacks may have had. It has been observed that the dietary needs of adult males, which were the concern of Fogel and Engerman, may not in fact be the same as those which contribute to good health among women and children. Kenneth and Virginia Kiple have argued that the African origins of black Americans produced three special dietary needs that must be recognized. The sickle cell trait that reduces the capacity of the blood to carry oxygen also reduces its capacity to carry iron, and so blacks need to have a diet which includes extra amounts of iron. A second characteristic which many blacks may have had emerges from the fact that West Africa is an environment in which cattle find it very difficult to survive. The result of this is that many West Africans have a weak capacity to digest milk effectively. In fact, seventy percent of adult blacks frequently develop indigestion when they consume milk. As a result, blacks frequently have a diet with a low intake of calcium, a mineral necessary to good bone structure and other aspects of good health. Furthermore, the intake of calcium among blacks in North America may have been further reduced because of low levels of vitamin D, a chemical that aids in the absorbtion of that mineral. Vitamin D is often acquired through the action of sunshine on the human body. Dark skin by and large does not produce vitamin D as effectively as light skin. In equatorial regions, where sunshine is both more intense and more constant the year round, dark skin is not a disadvantage. However, in more northerly regions, where sunshine is less strong, particularly during the winter months, the production of vitamin D among dark-skinned individuals may fall below necessary levels and hence reduce the intake of calcium.

In examining the diet of blacks in the first half of the nineteenth century, the Kiples discovered that the necessary levels of iron and calcium may well have been absent from the diet of Afro-Americans. In addition, they argue that the particular types of foods which planters frequently gave their slaves may have meant that certain slaves suffered from deficiencies in both protein and magnesium. Slave diets either did not provide sufficient amounts of protein, or in the case of cornmeal, the common element in the slave diet, did not provide protein in a useable form because slaves' bodies were unable to release that protein and absorb it in an efficient fashion. Ironically, some of the chemicals that are available to the body in pork, another staple of slave diets, actually work against the effective release and digestion of certain of the elements which would normally be available in cornmeal.

In addition to examining the actual level of dietary intake, the Kiples looked at plantation and runaway records that included descriptions of slaves and discovered, to their satisfaction, evidence of diseases that are directly related to the malnutrition which they found in the diet. Bone deformation, rigidity of certain muscles, distended bellies, and other characteristics which can be attributed to protein or calorie deficiencies, low levels of calcium intake, and insufficient amounts of magnesium in the diet are symptoms that are mentioned in the early nineteenth-century records. Thus, a knowledge of physical needs, of food chemistry, and an attention to the descriptions of blacks included in nineteenth-century records combine to suggest that at least one of the causes of lower life expectancy among nineteenth-century blacks was insufficient diet.

4. Longer Lives Since 1880—Why?

Since the mid-nineteenth century, Americans have experienced a dramatic improvement in life expectancy. Table VI presents one recently published set of figures for life expectancy at birth. Other estimates exist which differ slightly from those presented here. However, the differences reflected choices in methods of calculation and adjustments for errors, but do not in any way suggest a different overall pattern or a need to alter overall conclusions drawn from the data. In 1850, life expectancy at birth among the white population was in the neighborhood of forty to forty-two years. Black Americans had a life expectancy approximately ten years lower. By 1900, life expectancy among white Americans had increased notably. In that year, the life expectancy of white males at birth stood at 48.2 years; the comparable figure for white females was 51.1 years. Black Americans had not yet begun to show significant improvement in life expectancy so the figures for that part of the population in 1900 were perhaps no more than a year or two higher than those for 1850. By 1950, white males had a life expectancy of 66.3 years and white females showed a figure of 71.9 years. By this time, black Americans had begun to join their white counterparts in improved life chances with males having a life expectancy at birth of 58.7 years and females having a life expectancy of 62.4 years. Improvements in life expectancy have continued since 1950, though at a somewhat slower rate than before the period from 1900 to 1950.

Table VI. Life Expectancy at Birth, 1850–1968

	White		Non white	
Period	Male	Female	Male	Female
1850	40.4	42.9	—	—
1890	42.5	44.5	—	—
1900–1902	48.2	51.1	32.5	35.0
1909–1911	50.2	53.6	34.0	37.6
1919–1921	56.3	58.5	47.1	46.8
1929–1931	59.1	62.7	47.5	49.4
1939–1941	62.8	67.3	52.2	55.3
1949–1951	66.3	71.9	58.7	62.4
1959–1961	67.5	74.1	61.4	66.3
1968	67.5	74.9	60.1	67.5

SOURCE: S. L. N. Rao, "On Long Term Mortality Trends in the United States, 1850–1968," *Demography* 10 (1973): 412.

In addition to living longer now than ever before, Americans also die from different causes than were common in the past. One of the principal changes is a sharp decline in the number of deaths attributable to infectious diseases such as dysentery, typhoid, typhus, influenza, or tuberculosis. Contemporary Americans are much more likely to succumb to problems like heart disease, stroke, cancers, suicide, or accidents from gunshot wounds or automobiles. In many ways, Americans are their own worst enemies, inflicting serious damage on their bodies through their style of life and diet.

There is no doubt that significant improvements in life expectancy and dramatic changes in the causes of death have occurred since 1850, primarily after 1880. However, there is serious debate over what caused the change. Traditional medical history emphasizes that doctors became better able to cure diseases after 1880 than before. One reason for this was that medical education improved. A better biological understanding of the human body and of the causes of many illnesses was available after 1880. As a result, education improved not only because reformers insisted doctors take longer courses but also because their lessons had better content in them. Laboratory work became an important part of medical education only in the twentieth century. In addition, the technology available to doctors improved significantly, not only with such nineteenth-century inventions as the x-ray, anesthesia, and the practice of antisepsis, but also in the twentieth century when a remarkable explosion occurred in the drugs available to them. Such nonmedical technology as the telephone and automobile should not be overlooked in contributing to better health as well, because both of these inventions have made it possible for patients to get in touch with their doctors and receive care much more quickly than was the case in the past.

An emphasis on medical cures, however, is by and large misleading. Careful examination of the improvement of life expectancy makes it clear that, at least prior to 1920, preventive medicine, the things that kept people from getting sick in the first place, was much more important than medical cures. Figure 3 illustrates two important points regarding improvements in public health in this century. The first is that the control of major infectious diseases was tremendously

Figure 3. U.S. mortality rates and health care costs, 1900–1973.

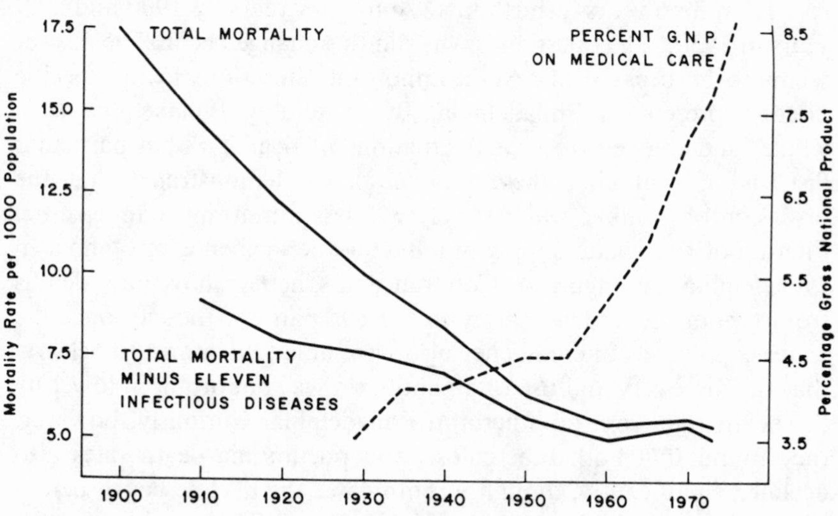

SOURCE: John B. McKinlay and Sonja M. McKinlay, "The Questionable Contribution of Medical Measures to the Decline of Mortality in the United States in the Twentieth Century," *Milbank Memorial Fund Quarterly* 55 (1977): 415. Reprinted with permission of the Milbank Memorial Fund.

important in longer life expectancy before World War II. The second is that the amount of resources devoted to better health and medical cures since 1955 may have helped people live better, but it has had only a small effect on how long Americans live.

Early efforts to understand the role of preventive medicine in the revolution in life expectancy emphasized particular reform movements such as those to improve the purity of milk, to include screens as part of summer housing, to improve water supplies in urban places, or to build privies in rural areas. Such studies tended to emphasize the contribution of individuals in bringing reforms. They were much less concerned with actually establishing what proportion of the change in life expectancy could be attributed to any single reform in Americans' health.

Recently, however, studies have been published which try to provide specific links between the introduction of a particular reform in a community and the decline in the death rate. Such studies depend upon precise chronology and the ability to specify when reforms were introduced into that community not only on the level of the whole community but even on the level of particular sections of town.

Gretchen Condran and Rose Cheney have demonstrated the value of this approach in their exploration of mortality trends in Philadelphia between 1870 and 1930. In Philadelphia, life expectancy rose from 39.6 years at birth in 1870 to 45.8 years by 1900 and 57.9 years in 1930. The question is why did this change occur. The answer seems to be because of several important alterations in the specific diseases present in Philadelphia. By examining Philadelphia as a whole, and the year-to-year fluctuations of deaths within particular districts of that city, these scholars have demonstrated that the provision of a public water supply was less important than eventual filtering of that water supply in reducing the incidence of typhoid in Philadelphia. In Figure 4, Condran and Cheney show how deaths from typhoid fever fell sharply in various parts of the city once the water supply was filtered. They also were able to demonstrate clearly that the discovery and use of an antitoxin was important in lowering the death rate from diphtheria in Philadelphia. Curiously, however, they found that both tuberculosis and pneumonia death rates also declined significantly, though in both cases the decline began before any readily discernible cause could be identified. Their explanation for this is simply a general improvement in the standard of living.

Obviously, to point to general improvements in the standard of living is not a very satisfactory way to explain as important a change as

Figure 4. Typhoid fever in Philadelphia, 1890–1920.

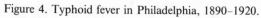

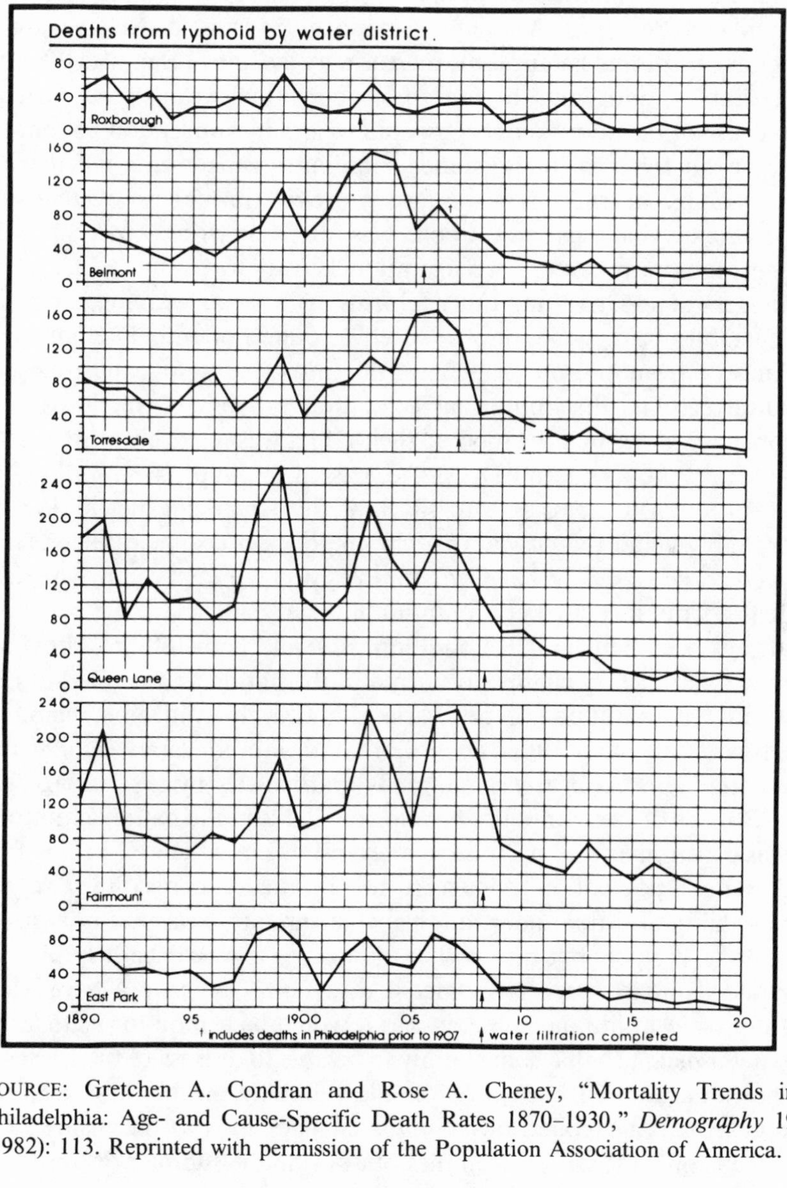

SOURCE: Gretchen A. Condran and Rose A. Cheney, "Mortality Trends in Philadelphia: Age- and Cause-Specific Death Rates 1870–1930," *Demography* 19 (1982): 113. Reprinted with permission of the Population Association of America.

the revolution in life expectancy. However, several new avenues of inquiry have recently begun to open up that offer some interesting possibilites in more precisely specifying what this meant to Americans in the last hundred years. It is known, for example, that the American diet changed significantly between 1880 and 1960. By and large, the number of calories that most Americans consumed declined and a better nutritional balance was increasingly available. Supplies of meat, vegetables, and fruits became more consistent year round, in part because of the invention of refrigeration and its application not only at home but also in long-distance shipping arrangements whether by railroad car or truck. Diet was also improved through efforts to assure Americans that the food they had was relatively wholesome. Since the late nineteenth century, refrigeration helped to eliminate the worst dangers of spoilage, and other reforms, as basic as washing fruits and vegetables before sale, have reduced, though not entirely eliminated, dangers from poisons ranging from insecticides to cancer-causing additives. The first important legislation providing Americans with some guarantee that the food on their tables was relatively pure was the Federal Pure Food and Drugs Act passed in 1906.

Although it seems safe to say that the American diet in 1980 is probably better than it was in 1880, there are still some questions that need to be raised. What, for example, was the impact on American health from increased consumption in meat, fats, and sugar? Has this always been beneficial? In addition, it would be helpful to know not only what dietary changes occurred in the nation as a whole but also whether consumption of food varies significantly by income, region, or ethnic backgound. It is possible that diet even varies significantly among members of the same family, particularly by sex and age.

Studies of the amount of housing available in the nation and how it was constructed also promise to offer insights into the well-being of the American population. A concern for domestic architecture raises the possibility of better understanding what sanitation was like not only in cities as a whole but also within the house. It would be helpful if we could demonstrate what it meant to a family to have a pure water supply piped into the home, just as it would be helpful for us to know what it meant to that same family to be able to dispose of the wastes of the home, not in backyards or alleys but by means of sewers and regular garbage collections. Simple changes such as the inclusion of screens on windows to keep flies out during the summer or improved ventilation may also have improved American health. Likewise, construction techniques which made it less possible for rats and mice to have close physical contact with human beings may also have improved American health. Here, too, there is a need to be aware of significant local variation in housing. The replacement of sod huts, which provided homes for all kinds of animals, with woodframe houses on the plains may not have had the same impact on health as the elimination of the worst of the urban slums in favor of tenement houses that had provision for significant ventilation. What also is the difference between the provision of sewers in northern cities and the construction of sanitary privies in rural communities in the South?

Careful studies of individual communities are needed in order to show how politics and economics affected the decision of individual towns to implement health improvements whose effectiveness had been demonstrated elsewhere. Economic historians like Edward Meeker have argued that significant investments in public health would have been more than repaid if nineteenth-century cities had undertaken them. Public health would not only have eliminated serious interruptions of trade during epidemics but also would have meant a healthier and more productive work force. Laborers would not have missed as many days of work if they had been healthier, and skilled workers would have had a longer life expectancy and so the training they acquired at some cost either to themselves or to their employers would have more than been paid back.

Interestingly, this relationship between spending on public health and the improvement of economic conditions in nineteenth-century cities was demonstrated as early as 1850, when a physician in New Orleans by the name of J. C. Simmons argued strenuously for public health improvements in that particular community. However, many southern businessmen refused to recognize the costs of ill health not only to their communities but also to themselves as individuals until after a disastrous invasion of yellow fever in many southern cities in 1878. Memphis, Tennessee, was one of the southern towns hardest hit during this epidemic. In that community, there were five thousand deaths out of a population of forty thousand; this figure is all the more dramatic considering that half the population fled Memphis at the onset of the epidemic. Nonetheless, after 1878 many southern cities, including Memphis, did respond by trying to provide regular sewage disposal, pure water, and some effort to clean the streets.

Twentieth-century concerns with effects of automobile and industrial pollution may lead us to have a somewhat idealized notion of the environment in nineteenth-century cities. It should be remembered, however, that animal traffic was constant in the city streets and that belief in minimal government meant that city residents were frequently responsible for disposing of their own wastes. Often this meant that garbage and human and animal wastes were simply tossed into alleys, left in the streets, or thrown into vacant lots. Needless to say, the fumes and smells of a nineteenth-century city must have been overpowering. Although the problem is not one that could easily be ignored, especially in the heat of the summer, communities like Milwaukee, Wisconsin struggled for almost thirty years over the problem of waste disposal. One question the city was unable to resolve satisfactorily was simply who was responsible for removing wastes. Was this a private matter or was the public interest at stake here? Even when this fundamental question could be satisfactorily resolved, issues arose over where and how garbage was to be disposed. Should incinerators be located within the community or should garbage dumps be built outside the bounds of the city limits? Should garbage be collected by public employees or should a monopoly be granted to private contractors to deal with this problem? These were some of the issues that Milwaukeeans debated in their efforts to come to terms with this major source of urban pollution and ill health.

Perhaps the most critical issues involving the health of nineteenth-century Americans who lived in cities involved the supply of water. Initially, the concern in most communities was simply to insure an adequate supply of pure water from some nearby source, whether this was a lake or a river. However, cities quickly discovered that as water supplies became more readily available through conduits and pipes, the problem of disposing of resulting waste waters became important, requiring not only the building of sewers but also providing some adequate outlet for those sewers which would not, in turn, contaminate either their own water supply or that of neighboring communities. Cities that were located on well-drained slopes near rivers frequently had little problem in providing adequate water supply and waste removal to their citizens. Other communities, such as Chicago, that were located in low-lying regions near lakes were forced to undergo major transformations before their problems with water were adequately solved. So severe were Chicago's natural disadvantages that the town ultimately had to relocate its water intake by digging a tunnel several miles out under Lake Michigan and reverse the flow of the Chicago River in order to provide adequate waste disposal. The city also laid sewers on top of the streets, covered the sewers, and raised many of the city buildings as much as twelve feet to the new street level. All this was necessary to provide better health for the city's residents.

Although future research will no doubt shed additional light on how other urban centers improved the health of their residents, we must not overlook the parallel decline in the death rate in rural America. This also requires further studies, because changes such as filtered water or the provision of sewers cannot explain improved life expectancy in agricultural communities. Advice was available to rural Americans about a wide variety of ways to improve their health, especially after 1900. The technology of how to build a better privy was circulated in the South with the aid of the Rockefeller Foundation. In addition, public health nurses brought information to rural families regarding how to improve diet, and means of insuring better child and maternal health as well. Vaccination was extended to rural populations via the public health nurses. No doubt housing changes also had an effect on improved life expectancy among farmers. Nonetheless, there are a series of important questions that remain to be explored ranging from what the building of drainage or irrigation ditches could mean in terms of the presence or absence of malarial mosquitoes to studies of the possible effects of the use of various agricultural poisons on farmers and their families. It is still unknown just how rapidly improved medical technology spread beyond major medical research centers into the heartland of America.

5. Defining Disease

Recently researchers have come to appreciate that meanings attached to disease, health, and death are often as important in determining how people respond to these matters as are the levels of mortality that maybe expressed in quantifiable terms. In this regard, the skills of the psychologist, anthropologist, sociologist, or philosopher are often more important than those of the demographer, biologist, or civil engineer. In the end, however, the insights of all these disciplines, and others, must be combined to provide a full understanding of the history of health and death in America.

One of the most basic, yet complex, historical problems involves the definition of diseases and how those definitions change over time. In order to explain how Americans ultimately came to eliminate many of the worst causes of illness and death in the last century, researchers must gain some understanding of what they considered to be sickness. Less often asked, but no less important, is the counterside of this question—what exactly is health? Are sickness and health opposites, such that the absence of one implies the presence of the other, or is something more involved?

In the last hundred years, the success of the germ theory of disease has led to an emphasis on specific causes for specific maladies. Prior to that time, however, doctors frequently had theories of disease which stressed one common cause of all illnesses. In the eighteenth century, for example, doctors generally defined health in terms of what was known as "homeostasis." This meant that a healthy body was a body in balance. By contrast, illness existed when the body was out of balance, whether that imbalance was caused by diet, drink, weather, or some other factor. Thus, in treating their patients, eighteenth-century doctors sought to return the body to balance. Sometimes this meant building up the body's vital forces; other times it could lead doctors to try to deplete what they felt to be too much energy in the physical system. This latter idea led to considerable use of bleeding in the late eighteenth and early nineteenth centuries as a means of reducing excess energy within the body's system. Similarly, it is easy to understand why nineteenth-century Americans found patent medicines that claimed to cure almost all illness appealing when they understood illness to be the result of only one underlying cause. If there was only one cause of all illness, then it was reasonable to assume that there might be only one cure. Obviously, it is important to understand assumptions about the cause of illness if some sense is to be made out of treatments that were provided or attitudes toward research for future medical cures.

As mentioned earlier, doctors in the past often were better acquainted with the symptoms of disease than with their specific causes. Frequently this meant that they confused different diseases with common symptoms and did not recognize that one disease might show several different symptoms as it progressed through its various stages. Even when symptoms were readily observable and were clearly associated only with one particular disease, they may not have been considered as a sign of illness if that symptom was common in the population. If health is simply an idea which involves being normal in the context of one's community, then a disease that is common in that community may not be recognized as something that can be eliminated. In the nineteenth century, tuberculosis was so prevalent in the American population that many people did not feel that it was in fact a treatable illness. It was simply something from which people suffered and died, but not anything that might legitimately be the object of prevention or cure. Medical historians have noted that epidemics that appeared irregularly, and admittedly in often spectacular forms, generally received much more attention from doctors and their patients than did the regular killers that were present on a year-to-year basis in the population. Frequently, these common killers accounted for such high proportions of the deaths in a community that they became an accepted part of life.

Sometimes physical suffering would be explained as the result of causes which prevented that suffering from being understood as illness resulting from disease. Throughout much of the nineteenth century, and in earlier periods as well, many diseases were explained not as sickness but as the result of sin or some inherent weakness of character. Thus, an individual suffered, not because he or she was sick, but because they had lived a dissolute life or were being punished by God. Under such circumstances suffering was not within the realm of medical care, but instead involved personal and spiritual reformation. Charles Rosenberg has shown that the cholera epidemic that swept over the United States from abroad in 1832 was initially seen as attacking only the poor or foreigners in American society. These individuals were seen as predisposed to the ravages of the epidemic either because of weak character or because God had some reason to wish to punish them. Under such conditions it is not surprising that communities took little or no effort to prevent the disease from spreading within their boundaries. By 1866, however, it was clearly understood that cholera was a communicable disease that struck not only the assumed inferior elements of society but also the upper classes. As a result, residents of American cities in particular undertook vigorous, if short-term, efforts to clean the streets and prevent the spread of what was clearly defined as an illness by that time.

Changing definitions of disease over long periods of time have led to some interesting responses to the suffering of individual Americans. In the eighteenth century, for example, hospitals were frequently little more than isolation units where individuals who were seen as needing to be separated from the rest of the community were placed. Frequently, victims of disease were lumped together with other undesirables in a general communal institution that functioned not only as a hospital but also as a workhouse, a house of correction, and an insane asylum. At the end of the nineteenth century, two diseases were widely recognized by doctors that either would not be considered as diseases today or would not be recognized at all. Masturbation was one such illness. This practice was assumed to cause a variety of problems among patients such as dyspepsia, urinary problems, epilepsy, blindness, dizziness, loss of hearing, headache, impotency, loss of memory, irregular heartbeat, general loss of health and strength, rickets, and nymphomania. Other symptoms doctors looked for were enlarged veins on the hands and feet, moist and clammy hands, stooped shoulders, pale sallow faces, and heavy dark circles under the eyes.

Neurasthenia was a disease that was assumed to afflict a number of Americans, but particularly middle-class women. The most common characteristic of neurasthenia was an ill-defined nervousness. However, this disease was assumed to have a variety of more specific physical manifestations ranging from profound mental and physical exhaustion to headache, ringing in the ear, odd tones of the voice, deficient mental control, bad dreams, insomnia, stomach disorders, muscle heaviness, blushing, restlessness, palpitations, vague pains, spinal irritation, impotency, hopelessness, claustrophobia, and fear of contamination.

Today no doctor would recognize either masturbation or neurasthenia as significant diseases. What has happened to them? Neurasthenia has simply disappeared as any kind of recognizable disorder. It has been replaced by a more sophisticated understanding of psychological behavior and a more sympathetic view of some of the stresses and strains of modern life. The case of masturbation is somewhat different. Initially, this particular activity was seen as a sin that was morally wrong. Today, it is generally accepted, if not necessarily as desirable, then at least as something that we need not worry about. In this case, the definition of masturbation as a disease seems to have been a halfway stage between behavior that was wrong because it was a sin and something that was acceptable. In its stage as a disease it was considered to be wrong, not for spiritual reasons, but because it was physically bad for an individual.

It should not be thought that the ebb and flow of definitions of diseases is a phenomenon associated with the past; it is worth keeping in mind that it is only recently that alcoholism has been defined as a disease rather than a weakness of character, and homosexuality has been defined as a matter of sexual preference rather than a psychological disorder. Pregnancy and childbirth have received intensive medical scrutiny in the twentieth century, suggesting that at least some doctors consider these conditions to be an abnormal, rather than a normal, part of female experience.

6. Doctors in Their Society

The relationship of doctors to their professional peers and patients plays an important role in determining what kind of health care is available to a community and how it is delivered. Ultimately, this will have an important effect on the level of life expectancy in society.

Medical history has often focused on influential and prominent physicians. A doctor like Benjamin Rush, who practiced in Philadelphia in the late eighteenth and early nineteenth centuries, has received considerable attention because of his contributions to medical theory and because of his interest in other political and social reforms. Rush's principal medical contribution, if it can be termed that, was to persuade many American doctors that bleeding was an effective treatment for individuals whose bodies had too much energy. Physicians such as William Osler and William Welch have received justifiable attention for their contributions in the early twentieth century in establishing the Johns Hopkins Medical School as the standard against which all other American medical schools should be measured. Harvey Wiley's efforts on behalf of the pure food and drug legislation and Henry L. Coit's efforts to insure a pure milk supply certainly deserve notice from students who wish to know why Americans' health standards improved.

However, to restrict our view to prominent and influential doctors fails to recognize that any adequate study of changing patterns of mortality must include the common doctors who lived in normal American communities, for it is important to understand the kind of treatment those doctors were able and willing to give their patients. Examinations of the regular, everyday practitioners of medicine have evolved along several lines.

The first of these demonstrates an interest in the origins and effectiveness of the medical profession. The reader will have already noted the evolution and improvement of medical education in the late nineteenth and early twentieth centuries. At the same time, licensing of doctors was once again introduced, allowing the medical profession to police itself more effectively. In the late eighteenth century, several states had permitted the licensing of physicians for the same purposes. However, by 1840, much of this early legislation had been repealed. Physicians who advocated bleeding and purging frequently were unable to establish claims that their medical practices were superior to the treatments offered by numerous nonlicensed dispensers of health care. In addition, some scholars have argued that the rising democratic spirit in the age of Jackson discouraged the granting of such privileges to any professional elite. In the mid-nineteenth century, many American doctors were active in the founding of the American Medical Association, and in the creation of permanent state and local boards of health, institutions that they were able to use to maintain standards and extend their influence in their communities.

At a time when physicians may be among the most trusted and influential members of their community, it is interesting to recall that this was not always the case. In Rochester, New York, in the nineteenth century, and in New England during the same period, doctors seemed to have played quite a different role in their society. Many regular physicians in the smaller rural communities were not well educated. They were highly mobile, at least in part because they were not widely respected at the time, and frequently had financial problems which stemmed either from a reluctance on the part of the population to use their services or a resistance to paying physicians for health care which did not in fact work very well.

Although doctors were not always the most prominent members of their community, they frequently reflected the values of the towns in which they lived. Thomas Bonner has demonstrated that from 1840 to 1940 Chicago physicians reflected many of the contemporary attitudes of the town remarkably accurately. Initially, Chicago doctors had a faith in progress and focused on individualism. They also had a good deal of regional pride which expressed itself in hostility to physicians from the eastern United States and Europe. At the end of the nineteenth century, Chicago doctors espoused conservative responses to increasing industrialization, in which they identified themselves strongly with other professionals such as bankers and merchants. After an initial rejection, they also enthusiastically adopted theories of Social Darwinism which expressed considerable contempt for the urban industrial poor. Eventually, physicians from the windy city responded to reform movements, strongly supporting a number of progressive reformers, especially in political affairs. By 1920, however, doctors began to revert to a more individualist theory of society and became advocates of self-interest. They were apathetic or hostile to social legislation, and became more concerned with their own individual enhancement and less interested in social reform.

The political and social issues of the 1960s and 1970s have generated an interest in how related problems might have affected medical care in the past. An interest in women's history, for example, has led to explorations of the admission of women into medical schools in the mid-nineteenth century, to a study of how male physicians struggled against female midwives to control the fees associated with pregnancy and childbirth, and to descriptions of how certain medical practices and diagnoses were influenced by the sex of the patient. Neurasthenia has already been mentioned as a disease associated with women in the nineteenth century.

The economic class of patients in the nineteenth century influenced the type of treatment that they might get, as it does today. Mental hospitals treated patients with considerable differences depending on whether they were prosperous or poor. Prosperous individuals frequently were able to afford individual attention, whereas lower-class patients were simply given custodial care. Likewise, early reactions to cholera depended, at least in part, on the economic standing of the individual. Poor people who got cholera were assumed for one reason or another to deserve the attack of such a disease. In 1832, the idea that cholera could also strike wealthy victims was so outrageous that upper-class individuals who were stricken by cholera were assumed to have some hidden character flaw that made them vulnerable. Only later was it realized that cholera made no distinction in terms of social class and hence medical care should be made available for what was increasingly perceived of as a disease rather than a sin. Obviously, however, prosperous Americans were better able to purchase medical care than were their lower-class neighbors, though given the medical care available in the mid-nineteenth century this was not always an advantage.

Although racial diffferences in life expectancy in the nineteenth century no doubt had complex roots in matters of diet, biology, and work, it is also true that racism may have affected the type of treatment that black Americans received. For example, at least one southern physician perfected an operation on the genital-urinary tract on female slaves before he performed the same surgical technique on white patients. After 1878, as many southern cities began to implement urban health reforms, such reforms were not always extended into lower-class or black neighborhoods.

The use of nonwhite patients as medical guinea pigs is a practice that has continued into the twentieth century. Birth-control pills were given their initial trial in Puerto Rico in spite of the fact that the pharmaceutical firms involved had headquarters in Massachusetts. The infamous Tuskeegee study described by James Jones, which ran from the 1930s into the 1970s, allowed southern black males with syphilis to live untreated so that doctors could see syphilis as it developed and ravaged human beings over a prolonged period of time. This medical experiment was particularly cruel because it could not in fact achieve its medical goals because most of the individuals admitted into the study had received some kind of minimal treatment for syphilis before they became a part of the experiment.

Attitudes of the sick toward medical care are often as important as attitudes of physicians in determining the kind of help that patients will receive. Historical studies by James Whorton, James Young, and others have demonstrated that Americans have frequently been willing to seek medical care outside the framework of professional medical practice, whether through patent medicines advertized in magazines, newspapers, or on the radio, or through the advice of individuals who offer medical cures at reduced rates. Patients have not always made the lives of doctors particularly easy as well. Individuals who are sick and experiencing the pain and uncertainty of ill health, and perhaps the fear of death also, frequently made extraordinary demands for attention on the lives of doctors. When their expectations are not always met, patients on occasion have refused payment to doctors, particularly in the nineteenth century when law courts were reluctant to grant doctors legal recourse in extracting fees. Even when doctors understood that the best medical practice would be to do nothing at all, patients' expectations about what proper medical care involved and their desire to justify the cost of medical attention has led them to pressure physicians to actively intervene. One interesting example is in the treatment of childbirth where nineteenth-century women encouraged doctors to control childbirth, if only to justify the cost of having a physician in attendance instead of a midwife.

The perspectives of philosophy and politics are also needed to understand the evolution of mortality in the nineteenth century, for both factors played a role in inhibiting the spread of medical knowledge and the adoption of new medical practices, which appeared, in some instances, quite threatening. Throughout much of the eighteenth and nineteenth centuries, medicine was frequently as much a philosophical system as it was an empirical science. Because such philosophical systems were very tightly structured, any empirical finding that might challenge a physician's understanding of one particular disease frequently also threatened his understanding of his whole medical practice. Scholars have condemned nineteenth-century doctors for being slow to adopt new findings, but they have neglected to set those new findings in the context of the philosophical assumptions those doctors held. The discovery of a specific cause for cholera, for example, required doctors not only to accept a new explanation for that one disease, but also to contemplate the idea that the whole homeostatic theory of medicine was possibly wrong. A life time of medical practice, during which life and death decisions had been made, was challenged by this major new discovery. In addition, it is frequently easier to see what new ideas were correct from the perspective of the twentieth century than it was at the time. In a period when there were lots of conflicting theories and new discoveries regarding medical practice, many of which ultimately did not prove to be effective, doctors quite reasonably remained skeptical and hesitant to adopt new techniques rapidly.

Increased sensitivity to the political preferences and skills of doctors may also contribute to our understanding of the medical care available to Americans. In the nineteenth century, a number of regional and national hostilities inhibited the exchange of improved medical knowledge and the adoption of better practices. Prior to the Civil War, physicians in the northern and southern parts of the United States were reluctant to give recognition to improvements which were made outside their region. American physicians frequently showed hostility to innovations that came from Great Britain, in particular, and Europe, in general. On a local level, physicians with political skills were frequently able to use newly established boards of health much more effectively than doctors who were insensitive to political realities of their community. In her study of Milwaukee at the end of the nineteenth century, Judith Leavitt describes one physician who was in charge of public health who proved so insensitive to the political needs of ethnic communities in the midst of a smallpox epidemic that he stimulated a reaction that led to the reduction in the authority of the board of health in that city.

7. The Meaning of Death

Death obviously involves major transitions for both the individual confronted by his or her own mortality and for surviving family and friends. Historians have only recently come to appreciate the wide variety of responses to death from one culture or time to another that gives human meaning to the statistical abstractions of the life table. Of special interest are the explanations of death offered by religion that provide differing degrees of comfort, the expectations that people had about the meaning and imminence of death, and the rituals and institutions which people have used to mark one of the two most basic of all life-cycle transitions (the other is, of course, birth). The relationship of the dying to the survivors also merits attention.

Underlying studies that focus on the comforts offered by religion to individuals who are dying is a question that arises from western dualism in which the body and soul are seen as distinct. The ultimate question involved here is simply what happens to the soul after death. As David Stannard has shown, seventeenth- and eighteenth-century

American Puritans had one of the harshest and most alarming views of the afterlife. They denied themselves the comfort that religion has often offered to individuals confronted with the end of their bodily existence. Puritans taught that although an afterlife existed, by and large most individuals would be condemned to punishment in hell rather than experience the rewards of heaven. Thus, although death was considered to be a release from life on earth which at the time was not terribly pleasant, most Puritans experienced considerable anxiety, if not fear, over whether they would be condemned to an eternity in hell or blessed with perpetual life in heaven.

In the nineteenth century, a number of authors began to write literature demonstrating to individuals how they should prepare for their own death. This material is particularly interesting not only because of the content involved in how one should prepare to die but also because Maris Vinovskis has suggested that the concern appears to be excessive when examined in the context of real levels of mortality. That is, given actual expectations of death, nineteenth-century Americans seemed to have anticipated death to be more imminent than it probably was. It is not entirely clear why this situation should have arisen, though it is possible that the continued presence of epidemic disease made it necessary for Americans to consider the possiblity of their imminent demise, even though the reality on a year-to-year basis often was otherwise.

Twentieth-century Americans demonstrate considerable ambiguities about death. Geoffrey Gorer has argued that death has become the great unmentionable, replacing sex as something that people do not discuss in polite company. It is also evident that Americans have increasingly removed themselves from the confines of their families when confronted by death, using hospitals as places to die. On the other hand, Elisabeth Kubler-Ross has received remarkable attention and approval for her efforts to define the stages that individuals go through when confronted with their own death, and to ease the transition from the denial of the possibility of their own mortality to ultimate peaceful acceptance of the possibility.

A basic question has emerged in the latter half of the twentieth century, primarily as the result of improved medical technology that has enhanced the doctors' ability to prolong life through various mechanical aids, that was never necessary to ask before. It is now necessary to ask: what is death? Throughout most of the past defining death was a nonissue, but it is certainly one of future interest. Is there some point at which mechanical aids become so important in sustaining the bodily functions of an individual that the person can truly be said to have died, or is it necessary for any evidence of heartbeat or brain activity to cease before a person can be said to be dead? It is ironic, given the long efforts of humans to control death, that at a time when death is remarkably under control that its exact nature is no longer known. As a result of the capacity of machines to sustain at least minimal levels of life, it may well be that we will have to give up our long-term search to avoid death, and in some instances actually welcome it. Perhaps historical efforts to understand the meaning of death in the past may contribute to our ability to answer fundamental philosophical and moral issues in the present and future.

Death affects not only the individual whose life is coming to an end but also surviving family and friends. The rituals and institutions surrounding death have histories of their own. Some of these involve short-term reactions to death and touch on the customs and surroundings of funerals, ranging over matters as different as the eighteenth-century habit of giving gifts, such as gloves, to members of the funeral party, to the theatrical productions staged in modern funeral parlors for the psychological, if not necessarily economic benefit of the survivors. Long-term efforts to commemorate the dead are also of interest. Burial grounds where the dead could be interred have evolved into park-like gardens with guarantees of perpetual care in cemetaries as widely separated as Mount Auburn in Cambridge, Massachusetts, and Forest Lawn in Los Angeles, California. The modern cemetary attempts to appeal to the living and not separate the dead into graveyards that had to be whistled passed. Headstone carving can be studied to gain insight into the human characteristic valued in different settings, and to determine a society's view of death from the engraved images. Skulls and doves clearly convey quite different messages, even though the meaning of the message may be open to interpretation.

It would certainly be possible to approach the topic of mortality in America from the narrow demographic concern with the risk of death of any individual or group of Americans. This alone requires the insights and techniques of a number of different disciplines such as demography, biology, and medicine. But to fully understand the subject from the perspective of people who lived and died under conditions remarkably different from those we face, it is necessary to become students of geography, psychology, culture, and society. It must be remembered that death, one of the most intimate of all experiences, also has complex meanings for family, friends, and society as a whole.

Chapter 4

Migration in American History

The Subject and Its Interest

Without much exaggeration it would be possible to say that American history is a history of migration. The first Americans arrived from Asia perhaps as many as 30,000 years ago and spread eastward across the continent. This movement was only part of a remarkable process, which involved the settlement of North and South America and many of the nearby islands, and produced an explosion of different cultures and languages in a remarkably short period of time. Thus, when the English arrived in 1607 to establish their first permanent settlement in Jamestown in Virginia, they planted their colonies in a land already subject to human endeavor and in the midst of cultures already interacting with each other, and frequently in the midst of groups of people who were in the process of moving themselves.

It did not take long for the English colonizers to realize that the Indian populations settled along the eastern fringes of North America were very small. This meant that they could not be exploited in the traditions of European colonization. Therefore, it would be necessary, if the English colonies were to be successful, to bring labor from abroad in order to make use of the abundant natural resources. From 1607 to the present, movement to America has been constant, though varying greatly in scale. The peak, of course, occurred between 1820 and 1920, as 30 million people arrived in the United States. Table VII provides data regarding the number of immigrants recorded entering the United States from 1820 to 1979.

Once here, European settlers did not remain long in one place. From cores of settlement around Massachusetts Bay, Narraganset Bay, the New York City and Long Island region, Delaware Bay, Chesapeake Bay, and the territory around Charleston, South Carolina, the initial English colonies expanded, first north and south along the Atlantic

Table VII. United States Population, 1790–1980

Year	Total Population (in millions)	Immigration in Decade before Census Year (in thousands)		Percent Urban
1790	3.9	N.A.		5.1
1800	5.3	N.A.		5.7
1810	7.2	N.A.		6.9
1820	9.6	N.A.		7.3
1830	12.9	152	(1820–1830)	8.5
1840	17.1	599		10.5
1850	23.3	1,713		15.0
1860	31.5	2,598		20.0
1870	39.9	2,315		24.8
1880	50.3	2,812		28.0
1890	63.1	5,247		35.0
1900	76.1	3,688		39.7
1910	92.4	8,795		45.5
1920	106.5	5,736		50.8
1930	123.2	4,107		56.0
1940	132.1	528		56.3
1950	151.7	1,035		63.6
1960	180.7	2,515		69.3
1970	204.9	3,322		72.9
1980	227.7	3,962	(1971–1979)	73.3

SOURCES: U.S. Bureau of the Census, *Historical Statistics of the United States, Colonial Times to 1970, Bicentennial Edition* (Government Printing Office, Washington, D.C., 1975), 8, 11–12; U.S. Bureau of the Census, *Statistical Abstract of the United States: 1982–83,* 103d edition (Government Printing Office, Washington, D.C., 1982), 25–26, 86.

coastline, and then gradually westward toward the Appalachian Mountains. Near the end of the eighteenth century, westward migration began to dominate, crossing first the Appalachians and then exploding over the rest of the continent, until the Pacific Ocean was reached by the middle of the nineteenth century. Whether they wanted to or not, black slaves accompanied their white owners west until the 1860s, and Indians contracted toward the Pacific in the face of the European expansion. After studying the results of the count in 1890, the Bureau of the Census officially announced that a frontier no longer existed within the United States.

The English colonies were not alone in their tendency to expand. During the seventeenth and eighteenth centuries, the Spanish placed settlements on the northern fringes of their empire, in territories that eventually became part of the United States. These settlements were scattered from Florida to Texas, through New Mexico and Arizona, and ultimately extended up into California in 1769. French migration out of the St. Lawrence into the Mississippi River Valley also occurred in the eighteenth century.

Until the twentieth century, the dominant movement within the United States was from east to west. However, around 1900, a significant number of black and white Americans began to move out of the South and into northern states. After World War II, southerners of both races moved increasingly to western destinations. In recent years, this flow has reversed, with many northerners moving south to what is called the "Sun Belt." To a lesser extent, some people living in the western part of the United States have moved back to the east.

Westward movement was not the only significant migration within the United States in the nineteenth century. Between 1790 and 1920 the country changed from a population that was five percent urban to one in which over fifty percent of the American people lived in cities of varying sizes, as is evident in Table VII. Urbanization began somewhat later than westward migration, but it may have changed the lives of more Americans in a more fundamental fashion than the expansion of farm communities. Although regions became urban at different rates, and cities varied dramatically in size, economic activity, and the people they attracted, the fact that today Americans are an urban people is surely as important to our history as our existence as a continental nation.

International, westward, and urban migration often have been treated as separate phenomena, but in fact they are closely linked. Polish or Italian peasants who moved to Chicago in the late nineteenth century clearly were involved in international migration, but they also were moving to a major city in the interior of the United States. Cities were frequently part of the frontier experience. Louisville, Cincinnati, and St. Louis all developed early in the process of white expansion into the upper Mississippi River Valley and the Ohio River Valley. San Francisco, Denver, and Salt Lake City offer parallels in the Far West. These urban areas not only attracted native-born Americans but frequently provided homes for immigrants from Europe. The motivations behind one person's move across the Atlantic were likely to be similar to those that led another individual to move from Ohio to Kansas or a third person to move from a farm into a city. Although we will not pursue the matter here, readers should keep in mind that America was only one of the many nations that received immigrants and underwent extensive urbanization during the nineteenth and early twentieth centuries.

The three themes of international, westward, and urban migration certainly deserve the notice they have received from historians and other students. However, there are complex local patterns of migration that command attention as well. Tamara Hareven has documented a definite pattern in the circulation of individuals and families from one New England textile town to another based on kinship networks and economic factors. Examinations by James Goldthwaite and others of residential patterns in several New Hampshire towns have demonstrated the importance of transportation in determining even the most local migrations. As roads or railroads were built or fell into disuse, the location of the most crowded parts of a particular community could change noticeably over one or two generations as people moved short distances to be close to the prevailing form of transportation. As ridge-running roads gave way to railroads in the valleys, the towns quite literally went downhill. Within Iowa during the nineteenth century Michael Conzen has discovered at least three distinct patterns of migration. Residents of Iowa were observed moving from east to west across the state, into the cities in the eastern section of the state, and to the capital of Des Moines from counties all over the state. Farther west, several particularly interesting local patterns of migration emerged. After their initial successful planting around Salt Lake City, Mormons began to expand southward within Utah, and ultimately into Arizona and Mexico. This expansion frequently involved a religious vision of a greater Zion. Studies of migration and residence within cities as different as Boston, Cincinnati, Omaha, Houston, and Los Angeles have demonstrated that every community had its own particular form of evolution.

It is not surprising that Americans have devoted considerable attention to migration as an important part of their history. Much of the concern is, of course, highly personal. Many Americans are still movers, and it is only natural to wonder how one's own experience compares to that of one's ancestors. The American dream of success is deeply rooted in the idea that the search for opportunities frequently involves the freedom to move. From the seventeenth century to the present, the ability to move geographically has been associated with the expectation of moving up the social ladder, as demonstrated in studies by Russell Menard, Stephan Thernstrom, Peter Knights, and others ranging from explorations of how many indentured servants in the seventeenth century were able to significantly improve their status once they were free, to examinations of the origins of the business leaders of

Seattle in the early twentieth century. Even when dreams of success are not vitally important to an individual, migration can still be of considerable interest, because all Americans are ultimately descendents of immigrants, though some have ancestors who arrived more recently than others.

Concerns of broad historical and social significance have caused students to ask questions that have led them to the study of migration. Given the volume and variety of migration to the United States, and within the country as well, students have asked whether the history of America can be written only in political and, perhaps, economic terms. Is there also a valid history of the American people, or are Americans too divided by region, race, religion, and culture? The answers to these questions play an important role in determining not only how one interprets the American past but how one envisions the American future.

In practice, the answers to these questions have provided two opposing interpretations of American history, both of which date from the eighteenth century, if not before. One view is that migration has produced social fragmentation and dangerous instability. Migrants or their descendants already in America frequently have feared that new groups or individuals will not share basic values regarding God, family, or the use of land, and hence will disrupt the community, the state, or perhaps the nation. In the seventeenth century, New England towns controlled who was permitted to stay and who had to leave. In the twentieth century, immigration restriction became part of the national law.

During the nineteenth century, biological theories anticipated the possible deterioration of the American people in the face of immigration. Some of these theories were tied to environment. One such view, advanced originally in the late eighteenth century by the Comte de Buffon, a French scientist, asserted that the wild and large scale of the American environment threatened not only the health and physical development of individual Americans, but also presented a danger to their ability to maintain proper cultural and political controls. In the latter half of the nineteenth century, theories involving race led individuals, especially those whose families had long been present in this country, to express fears of possible race suicide or of a weakening of American society produced by impurities introduced by new immigrant groups. These theories were developed most elaborately in the first two decades of the twentieth century in books and articles, such as Madison Grant's, *The Passing of the Great Race,* or Crum's, "The Decadence of the Native American Stock" (discussed in chapter

2). Such works often included confused links between biology and culture in which certain racial types were assumed to be better equipped to handle democratic forms of government and free economic competition. Other groups, particularly those represented by new immigrants, were deemed more inclined toward oppressive forms of government and inappropriate modes of economic organization.

In striking contrast to these fears and anxieties is an interpretation of immigration that celebrates the differences of the American people and values immigration as a source of strength to be encouraged rather than of weakness to be opposed. Even the titles of Carl Wittke's, *We Who Built America,* or Oscar Handlin's, *The Uprooted: The Epic Story of the Great Migrations that Made the American People,* suggest the fundamental difference between their interpretation and that of Grant and Crum. Common expressions of this particular view involve catalogues of contributions by various ethnic groups to American society. These studies often have been produced by immigrants or their children interested in demonstrating the contribution of their particular ethnic group to American society. Such studies have included not only demonstrations of economic contributions, but also assertions of attachment to America, counts of how many individuals volunteered to serve the country in times of war, and even lists of words contributed to the American variety of the English language. This approach has described Americans as a new people emerging from a melting pot, including the best parts of all the old. Others, of course, have used the melting pot metaphor to raise alarms about the production of an alloy involving the worst parts of all Americans. However, numerous studies have demonstrated that the foreign born brought new skills, attitudes, energy, and a deep commitment to the American dream.

The concern about whether there is an American history or only histories of Americans is most visible in studies involving international migration. However, explorations of internal migration, either to the west or to the cities, include this theme as well. The origin, persistence, and significance of regional differences rooted in complex patterns of internal migration have been the object of sophisticated studies ranging from John Stilgoe's examination of preindustrial America to Raymond Gastil's descriptions of present differences.

Studying Migrations: Definitions, Theories, and Sources

The actual task of studying migration is rather complicated, partly because of the emotions involved, but also because of the subject itself and its sources. Although the primary purposes of the discussion below are to define the nature of migration, outline its theories, and comment on its sources, we can also reflect in passing on several of the traditional historic questions regarding who moved, where they went, how they moved, why they moved, and with what results. Intensive discussion of several new and relatively unexplored themes involving migration in American history will be undertaken in the final section of this chapter.

1. Definitions

We can begin with a simple question, who is a migrant? A migrant is obviously someone who has moved, but that quickly raises questions about how far have they moved and how long they intend to stay.

The question of distance in migration is not as simple as it may seem on the surface. Few would see a move across a street or to a different apartment in the same building as migration, though such moves may reflect major changes in a family's need for space or in an individual's ability to afford a penthouse rather than a basement apartment. To the extent that such short-distance moves result from dramatic changes in social status, they perhaps should be considered as migration. Even somewhat longer distances raise questions about interpreting the significance of migration. Imagine two Illinois farm families in the nineteenth century living somewhere west of Chicago. One of these families moves twenty miles east into Chicago. The other moves 250 miles west to another agriculatural community in Iowa. Which has changed the most? Has one migrated a greater distance than the other, and if so, is the greater distance spatial or cultural?

A common measure of migration demographers use is simply one involving the crossing of a border to a different political entity whether nation, state, county, or town. However, movement across a political border may not involve a long physical distance or a fundamental change in life. In the nineteenth century, farm families moved north and south along the valley of the Red River of the North, passing through several states and crossing the United States-Canadian border. Nonetheless, most of these families remained within a fundamentally similar environment from which they sought to earn a living by raising wheat. Conversely, immigrants to ethnic ghettos in nineteenth-century American cities may actually have experienced greater dislocation before they moved to the United States if they left their farms in the old country to move to cities in Europe before crossing the Atlantic. Such individuals might well have been protected from the need to learn a new language by living among their fellow natives, but could not avoid being involved in the new rhythms of urban life and activity. The point of this is that distance may frequently be as much a cultural as a physical or political phenomenon, though the former is much harder to measure than the latter.

It should also be noted that distance is very closely related to time. Moving thirty miles in the seventeenth century may have erected as effective a barrier to visiting one's family and friends as a five-hundred mile automobile trip or a flight of thousands of miles by airplane. A journey in 1800 from Massachusetts to Ohio may have separated individuals more completely than migration from Massachusetts to Australia would today. Because migrants often moved more than once over the course of a lifetime, a series of short moves might accumulate to a large distance and might also include residence in several widely differing environments.

In studying migration, it is also of interest to ask how long someone must stay in a particular community in order to be considered a migrant. Is a month sufficient, or is it necessary to stay a year, or perhaps even a decade, in order to be considered a migrant rather than a visitor? If, after a short residence, individuals move on to a new community, they surely would be considered migrants, but what happens if they return home? Do we then consider them visitors or were they, in fact, migrants to the first community for a short period of time? These questions are not easily resolved.

Is a commitment to remain also important in a judgment about how long someone needs to stay in order to be considered a migrant? In the nineteenth and early twentieth centuries, Irish Catholics and Russian Jews came to the United States expecting to stay. In contrast, British and Italian industrial workers often moved back and forth across the Atlantic several times in the course of their lives. Some people came to America at relatively young ages but expected ultimately to retire to their homelands after spending twenty or thirty years earning a living in the relatively prosperous North American cities. These individuals might be judged as migrants with regard to their impact on the American economy, but could be considered as visitors in terms of cultural or political involvement. The young women who labored in the Massachusetts milltowns of the early nineteenth century may have intended to stay only a short period of time in places like Lowell before returning to the country, but they surely were not the same people after their experience in a milltown as they were before they left home. Were these young women migrants or were they not? When did the women who abandoned plans to return home and committed themselves to an urban lifestyle become migrants?

Recognizing that defining a migrant or migration is not always an easy task, it is useful to examine some of the theories and sources that have been used to study migration in the past.

2. Theories

Theories of migration are concerned in general with who moves and why, because migrants never form a perfect cross section of the territory they are leaving or of the communities to which they are going. In their simplest forms, most theories of migration can be reduced to explanations involving push and pull. This means that migrants are to some extent pushed from the communities in which they have been living by various unfortunate circumstances, ranging from low wages, to religious or political persecution, or to an unhappy family life, and are pulled or attracted by the place to which they are going by some other set of circumstances, which may include higher wages, greater perceived economic or religious freedoms, and a chance to start one's life over again. This basic push-pull model is more sophisticated than it initially appears because it involves recognition not only of the importance of the migrant as an individual but also recognizes the need for a student to concentrate on both the territory sending the migrant and the region to which the migrant is moving.

There are several additional observations that deserve to be made about push-pull theories. Push and pull frequently can be divided into objective observations that either the migrant or the student of migration can make about the communities involved, and those observations that are really more mythological. Many migrants frequently had incomplete knowledge and a highly distorted image about where they intended to move, and in some cases even about their own community. Thus, their decision to move may or may not appear rational to the student of migration.

This simple model of migration can be made somewhat more complicated by introducing the concept of an *intervening variable*. What this means is that between the community a migrant is leaving and the place where he or she is going are a series of obstacles that may hinder the journey, and various factors that may make a trip easier than it might have been twenty years before, or might make a trip to one community easier than a journey of the same physical distance to a different place. Easily identified intervening variables include: geographic features such as mountains, oceans, or rivers; legal restrictions; borders at which customs have to be paid; and the availability and cost of transportation. However, intervening variables can also include unexpected alternatives encountered en route, such as new information about the proposed destination that encourages an alternative choice, the unexpected attraction of a community where one stops along the way, or perhaps even something as basic as encountering a potential spouse that leads to marrying and settling down before the original goal is attained. Alternatives can both encourage and discourage migrants in their efforts. Obviously, the longer the journey the greater the opportunity for intervening variables to appear and alter the original goal.

Over the course of the last century, several students of migration have attempted to establish laws or sets of hypotheses about migration. In 1885 and 1889, E. G. Ravenstein, a British scholar, published some influential hypotheses about migration. His more important generalizations include the following propositions. Net migration is always a small proportion of the gross migration between two areas. This means that the shift in total population between two places caused by migration is frequently much smaller than the total number of people who move between the two communities during a given period of time. In terms of a single place, overall growth from migration is generally much smaller than the total number of people who move into and out of the community in question. Ravenstein's first proposition is closely linked to his second, which is that every current of migration from one community to another frequently has a counter current moving in the opposite direction. Ravenstein also observed that migrants generally move only a short distance at any one time, but that the same migrants often travel much longer distances by a sequence of stages. For example, migration from rural to urban environments may occur by moving first from farm to town, then from town to small city, and finally from a small city to a larger city. Ravenstein also observed that migrants, at least in Great Britain in the 1880s, were more often female than male.

In 1966, Everett Lee provided a number of additional observations on migration. One of his first points was that migration is selective; that is, migrants do not represent accurately either the community of their origin or the community of their destination in terms of age, sex, race, or economic standing. Furthermore, the selection of migrants involves the push factor at the point of origin, as well as the elements attracting migrants at the destination. Lee also observed that selection increases according to the difficulty of the intervening obstacles involved, and is very closely connected to certain stages of the life cycle of the migrants.

Lee also made several observations about the volume of migration. First, the volume of migration depends on the amount of diversity within the areas from which and to which migrants are going. In addition, the volume of migration is related to the difficulty of the intervening variables and those same variables will affect the size of the stream of migrants eventually returning home. According to Lee, the volume of migration frequently depends heavily on fluctuations in the economy, with larger economic differences between place of origin and destination producing larger streams of migration. Regions of similar economic outlook will not have extensive exchanges of population.

Many theories of migration, including those of Ravenstein and Lee, are ultimately based on economic considerations. Some of these assume rational economic judgments on the part of the migrants in which individuals actively assess whether their economic opportunities are better served by staying at home or moving. On the other hand, some economists argue that economic structures can change in fundamental ways, forcing more passive individuals out of particular territories and into new regions. For example, Neil Fligstein's study of migration out of the American South in the twentieth century has demonstrated that structural changes in the nature of southern agriculture, involving the increased use of machinery, meant that many southerners, both black and white, were suddenly unemployed and found it necessary to leave the South in order to find employment. Ironically, increased use of machinery in northern urban areas provided these individuals with opportunities to find work in factories.

Not all theories of migration are at heart economic. Some draw parallels between physical phenomena and movements of population. Gravitational models have been advanced that express the amount of migration between any two communities in terms of their relative size and the distance separating them. Migration also has been linked to the theory of a demographic transition in which the decision of a migrant to move is seen as a demonstration of that individual's determination to seize control of his or her own life and to seek out a better existence elsewhere. Obviously, "better" in this theory frequently is defined in economic terms, but it need not be exclusively economic.

Another theory of some interest involves the interaction of culture and geography. Geographers have put forth the idea that any region undergoing a process of new settlement or resettlement will pass through a stage in which the first effective settlement is established.

This means that at some point in time a group with a particular set of cultural characteristics will come to dominate and define a given community. Thereafter, migration to that community tends to be extremely selective, so that individuals who would not be comfortable with the values and attitudes of the people who already live there will not go there. Conversely, individuals who are attracted by the values, attitudes, and style of life of a particular region will be unusually encouraged to move there. Dorothy Johansen has suggested that the farmers who went to Oregon attracted quite a different type of follower than the men who went to California in search of gold. Mormon domination of Utah is another example of this process at work.

Scholars have also linked migration to the life cycle of individuals, observing that decisions to move are not always the result of rational economic choices but may be the unanticipated consequences of basic changes in a person's life such as being married, having a child born into the family, or experiencing the death of one's parents or spouse. Such major changes can either encourage or in some cases force an individual to leave his or her old home for a new environment. Newly married women who moved to their husband's town in seventeenth-century Connecticut and twentieth-century urban couples who bought houses in the suburbs when their first child was born have both engaged in similar behavior.

One set of theories of interest here are concerned not with general patterns and causes of migration but with its effects on American society. Perhaps the most famous theory in this area is that of Frederick Jackson Turner. Expounded in 1896, it asserted the importance of the American frontier. Put simply, Turner believed that the existence of a frontier in American society presented opportunities for the country that were fundamental in directing its political and economic development along democratic paths. Turner feared that the end of the frontier would redirect American society in ways that were not entirely clear, but which he felt were not likely to be beneficial to the nation. Turner's views have been revised and altered since he first advanced them, but they still remain an important element in studying American history.

Numerous students of American history have argued at length over the significance of large numbers of immigrants from abroad and the existence of sectional differences in America produced, at least in part, by selective migration. Such scholars frequently have been more concerned with what they believed ought to be going on within American society than with describing what actually had happened in the American past. Of special interest has been the effects of new groups on already established society.

A number of alternatives have been suggested, though which one is correct is not yet clear. We have already noted the perspective of America as a melting pot in which old and new cultures come together and are somehow heated and refined into some entirely new alloy. Other scholars argue that the melting pot does not, in fact, exist and that any blending that occurs is frequently incomplete. Some suggest that new immigrants adjust to American society and are able to function within the legal, economic, and political systems without giving up their more fundamental cultural values. A second possibility is that once effective settlement is established new arrivals must accommodate themselves to the already dominant groups either by conforming to the established patterns or by discarding their older values and becoming, in effect, a native, white American, a northerner, an urbanite, or whatever.

A final set of theories about the importance of migration in American history has emerged from recent efforts to establish links between geographic and social mobility. Scholars such as Thernstrom have explored the question of how often individuals who moved up and down the social ladder frequently were geographically mobile as well. Although the two are not necessarily linked, individuals who prospered in communities as different as Boston, Massachusetts, Trempeleau County, Wisconsin, or Rosebud, Oregon, often remained in that community longer than those who did not find opportunity. This was especially true in the nineteenth century. Curiously, since World War II, patterns of mobility in American society seem to have reversed so that the most mobile Americans, at least in terms of long distance moves, are now those with the greatest education and the highest economic standing.

3. The Sources and What They Tell Us

The sources available to students of migration in American history deserve attention, in part because they are quite varied and need to be examined separately. In addition, studies of migration in the past frequently have depended on only one or a limited variety of sources, and this has influenced the possible questions and answers. The particular emphasis and interpretation of an author is, thus, a combination of the initial stimulus to investigate a topic and the kinds of evidence that the sources provide. We will focus here both on what has been done and what can be done with various kinds of documents.

Statistics collected and made public by various governments are among the important sources of information for students of migration. The federal government has been responsible for collecting demographic data since 1789. One of the most important is the series of statistics on immigrants recorded since 1820. This data series provides yearly evidence on the number, age, sex, and occupation of people moving to the United States. It is necessary, however, to keep in mind that these data are not always as reliable as they appear. Frequently immigrants were recorded only if they arrived at major ports of entry such as New York, Philadelphia, or New Orleans. Migrants who arrived at smaller ports up and down the Atlantic or Pacific seacoasts might have escaped note. Similarly, individuals who landed in Canada and then entered the United States by land from the north were not always counted.

The information about any particular individual was also subject to error. The sex of each migrant probably was recorded with reasonable accuracy. Age would be subject to greater interpretation, though obviously a child could be distinguished from a young adult, and a young adult would in turn clearly be different from an old person. Data on occupation, however, were probably subject to considerable error. Individuals arriving in the United States would be asked what was their occupation. Their reply, often in a language not fully understood by the immigration officials, might reflect what they hoped to become in the United States rather than what they were in the old country. It is also true that immigrants from abroad might have left a farm and moved to a city in England, Denmark, or Italy, where they acquired an urban occupation. Thus, someone moving to the United States might have skills in two or more fields, and yet be recorded as having abilities only in one particular area. This is especially important for anyone interested in examining the nineteenth-century immigration statistics in order to determine what the economic gain to the United States was from allowing millions of immigrants to move to this country.

Immigration statistics can be supplemented by a wide variety of documents. One important, yet overlooked, set of data includes statistics on emigration that began to be recorded only toward the end of the nineteenth century, possibly because Americans were not initially as interested in those individuals who desired to leave their country as they were in those people who found America an appealing place full of opportunity. In addition, many European countries kept track of the numbers of people leaving and where they said they were going. These data can be used to check the accuracy of American records. Frequently there are considerable discrepancies between the numbers of individuals recorded as leaving a European country for the United States and the numbers of individuals from that particular nation arriving in America in any given year.

For the years prior to 1820 immigration statistics are not readily available. Nonetheless, we are not completely without records for this period. As early as the seventeenth century, the English government took steps to register indentured servants who were leaving for the American colonies. These lists have enabled Abbot E. Smith, David Galenson, and others to describe the surprisingly large numbers of men and women who moved to the English colonies under the bonds of a servant's contract. Similarly, ship captains were occasionally required to keep lists of those people on board their vessels who were traveling to America. These can supplement official immigration statistics.

The federal censuses taken every ten years from 1790 to the present are a second source of considerable importance in the study of migration. State and local censuses supplement the national information in some locations. Whenever it is possible to estimate birth and death rates, and hence calculate the rate of natural increase for a particular region, any discrepancy in the census above or below the anticipated population total can be attributed to migration. For example, if we know that births exceeded deaths in New York State by a million over a given ten-year timespan, but the difference between the censuses at the start and finish of the decade in question show a growth of only 800,000 individuals, then we can conclude the New York lost 200,000 people through migration.

In 1850, the federal census began to record the place of birth for every individual living in the United States and published these data by place of residence. This information has proven useful to students of both international and internal migration. An example of one of the simplest uses for this evidence is the kind of study which might report the number and/or proportions of people living in Indiana, in 1870, who were born in New York, Pennsylvania, England, Germany, Ireland, or other places.

These data can provide much more detailed pictures of migration patterns, however. Making use of the manuscript census returns to examine where the children in families were born has allowed scholars to trace the routes by which those families arrived at the place they were living when the census was taken. Communities from Texas to Oregon have been shown to have derived their inhabitants from families in which the husband and wife might have been born in Virigina and Pennsylvania, respectively, and whose first child might have been born in Ohio, the second in Indiana, and a third in Missouri before the family moved on to the state in which they were recorded. Figures 5 through 7 show several ways this data can be used. Figure 5 indicates the routes by which people from various parts of the United States moved into East Texas and suggests the extent to which such groups settled in separate communities. Figure 6 shows the various paths used by families who started out in New York who arrived in Oregon's Willamette Valley by 1850. Figure 7 demonstrates not only that Oregon's immigrants frequently came from Missouri, but also that many of them, whether adults or children, had ties to a wide variety of states lying east of the Mississippi.

Although this type of evidence is tremendously important in demonstrating the number of short-distance moves that people undertook, it nonetheless records only the minimum level of migration in American society. Evidence of movement on the part of a married couple depends upon the birth of a child in a particular location. A couple moving from Pennsylvania to Texas might actually have stopped in several states on the way, but there would be no evidence of such a stay unless a child was born who was still living at home at the time of the census. It is also true that the place of birth is recorded by state only. Thus, two children recorded as having been born in Illinois could have been born in two separate locations in that state, but that would not show up in the census records. Therefore, such documents give us very little chance to understand movement within a state. A migrant from upstate New York to New York City would not be apparent from this kind of record, because he or she would simply be recorded as having been born in New York and still living in New York. In some regions, state censuses are helpful in studying more local patterns of migration.

The examination of data on place of birth has been important for understanding what migration meant to particular communities in a variety of ways. By distinguishing between the place of birth of adults and the place of birth of children, it has been possible to determine more accurately the influence of particular cultural streams on particular communities. For example, although midwestern towns in the middle of the nineteenth century were dominated by native-born Americans, close examination of census records indicates that foreign-born individuals were in the majority in the adult population. In Burlington, Iowa, in 1860, for example, over half the adult males

Figure 5. Texas migrations and colonizations, 1830s–1860.

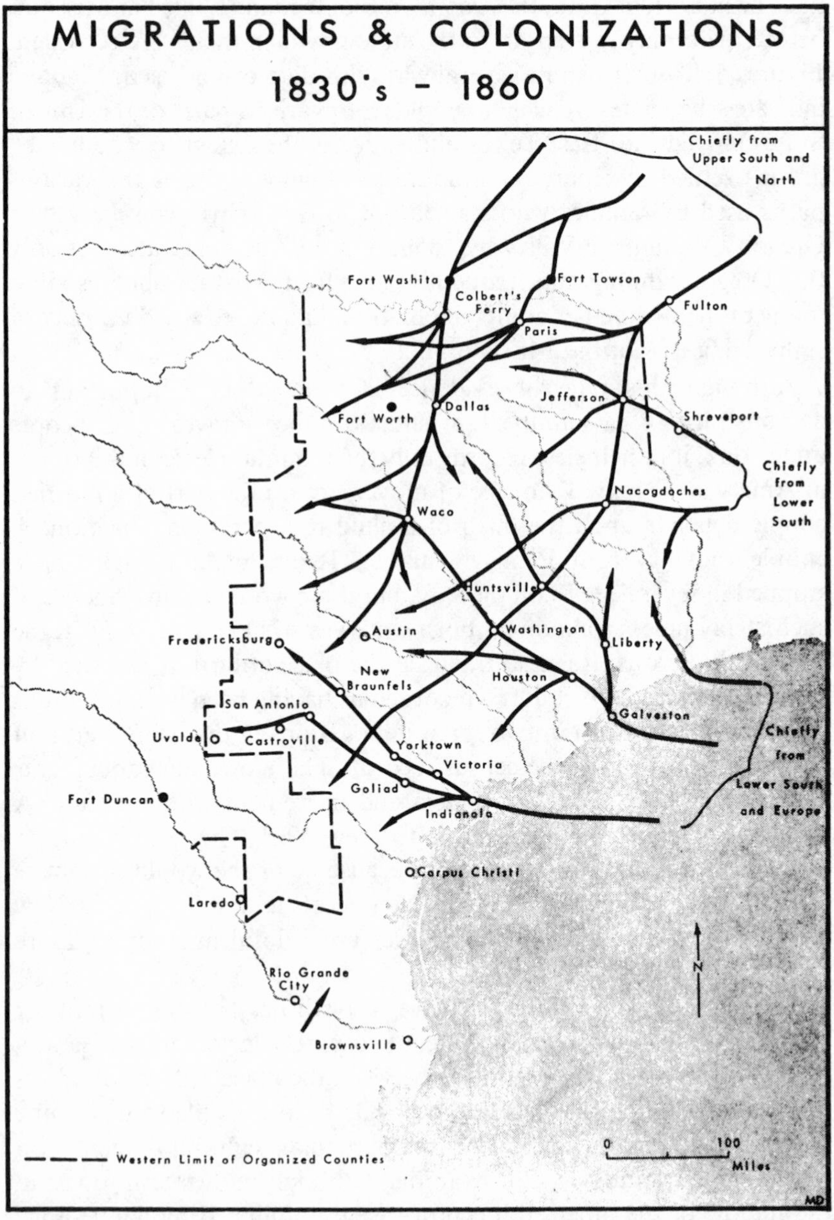

SOURCE: Donald W. Meinig, *Imperial Texas: An Interpretive Essay in Cultural Geography* (Austin, Tx.: University of Texas Press, 1969), 44. Reprinted with permission of the University of Texas Press.

Figure 6. Diffusion of New York families migrating to Oregon.

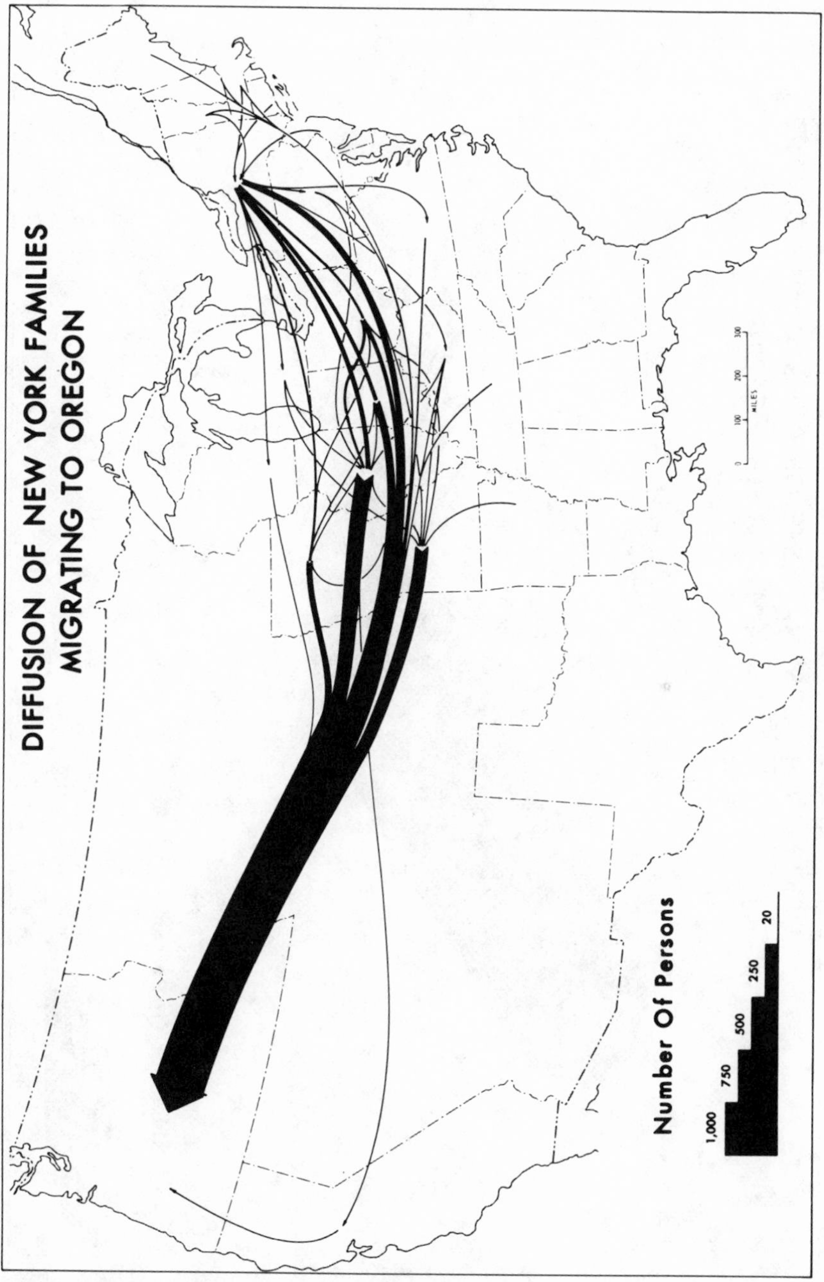

SOURCE: William A. Bowen, *The Willamette Valley: Migration and Settlement on the Oregon Frontier* (Seattle, Wa.: University of Washington Press, 1978), 37. Reprinted with permission of the University of Washington Press.

Figure 7. Origins and destinations of Oregon immigrants passing through Missouri.

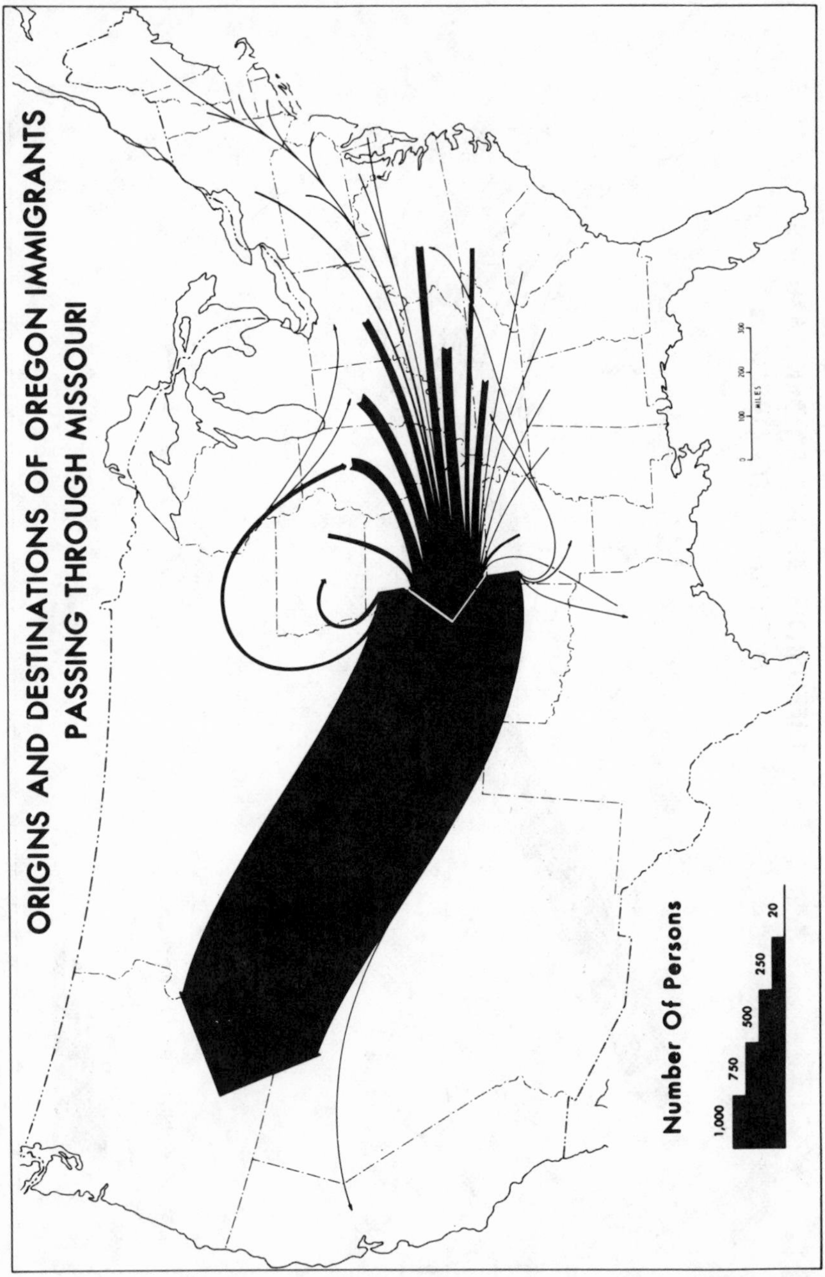

SOURCE: William A. Bowen, *The Willamette Valley: Migration and Settlement on the Oregon Frontier* (Seattle, Wa.: University of Washington Press, 1978), 34. Reprinted with permission of the University of Washington Press.

(voters) were foreign born, even though two-thirds of the inhabitants of the community had been born in the United States. This has considerable consequences since foreign-born voters often showed strong preferences for Lincoln in that year. The association of the foreign born with particular parties was common throughout the nineteenth century, although the preferences of the New York Irish in 1840 offer little help in predicting Irish political choices in California in the 1850s.

In the early years of settlement large numbers of Oregon's inhabitants came from Missouri or Illinois. However, detailed study indicates that many of the inhabitants from those states were in fact the children of parents who had originally come from New York, Virginia, or Kentucky. These conclusions emerge from both Figure 7 and Figure 8. The age and sex characteristics of the Oregon population by place of birth, presented in Figure 8, make it clear that many of the children in Oregon had been born either in that state or in Missouri or Illinois. In contrast, older Oregonians, especially males, frequently came from states farther east. Thus, instead of automatically interpreting the evolution of Oregon society in terms of a predominantly midwestern influence, it is essential to consider whether Oregon was, in fact, more a cultural offshoot of the eastern upper South and New York.

One common use of census documents in the last fifteen to twenty years has been to determine the *persistence* of individuals in a community over the span of a decade. The primary interest in such studies has been to link individuals who remained in nineteenth-century communities with records of economic and social standing to see what, if anything, distinguished those who remained from those who moved on. This kind of study records not only the social mobility, upward and downward, of individuals within a community, but also tells us a great deal about a community's stability. As results have accumulated, one of the most important conclusions to emerge has been that persistence was surprising low in nineteenth-century communities, whether they were located in the East or the West, or were rural or urban in nature. Frequently, less than half the population living in a particular town in one year would still be there a decade later.

There are some problems involved in using this kind of material that need to be kept in mind in assessing the findings. One of the most obvious difficulties is that it is impossible to determine from the census records alone whether an individual who disappeared in the space of ten years migrated or died because of an epidemic or old age. In

Figure 8. American population of Oregon: Age-sex characteristics by state or territory of birth.

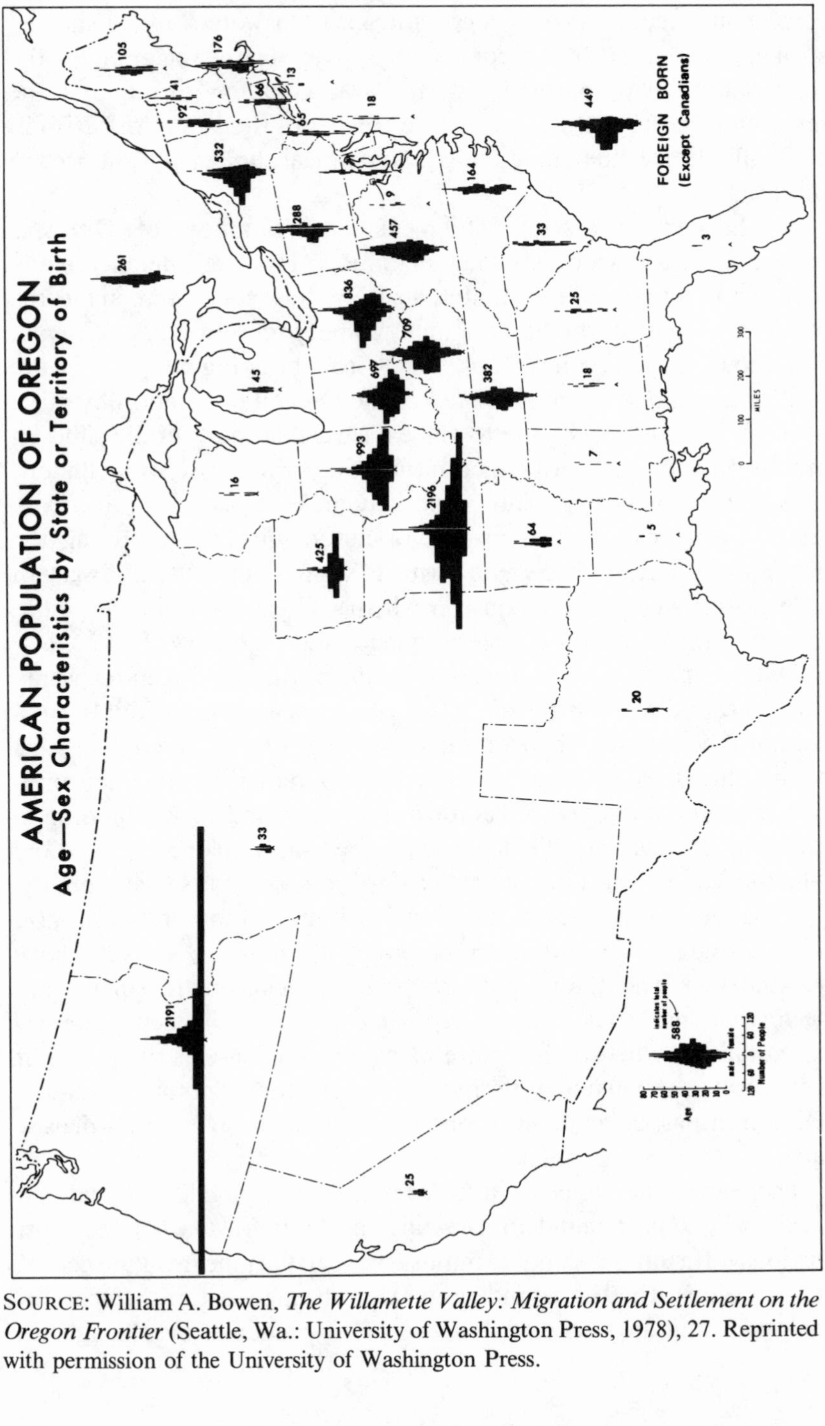

SOURCE: William A. Bowen, *The Willamette Valley: Migration and Settlement on the Oregon Frontier* (Seattle, Wa.: University of Washington Press, 1978), 27. Reprinted with permission of the University of Washington Press.

addition, there is no way to track down anyone who moved in after the initial census was taken but moved away before the next census was taken. Thus, there may be considerable movement in and out of a community that the decennial censuses never recorded. A third problem involves the fact that censuses provided better evidence on the migration patterns of men than women. Because women generally change their last names when they marry, it is often impossible to know whether a woman who disappears from a community has moved, died, or simply changed her name through marriage. If men and women migrated at the same rates and in the same directions this would be no problem. However, it is clear from studies based on other sources that in both the twentieth century and earlier periods male and female migration patterns are generally not the same.

Because census records are more prone to lose track of poorer individuals than more prosperous residents of the community, it is probable that an undetermined amount of class bias exists in studies of persistence. Here, too, this is of some consequence, because the evidence indicates that economic prosperity or poverty played an important role in determining how quickly individuals decided to move from a particular place. This is especially interesting in view of the fact that the nineteenth century trend for the poor to move and the prosperous to remain in one place seems to have shifted in recent years as well-to-do Americans have become relatively more mobile than their poorer neighbors, especially over long distances. Any bias in the records distorts our ability to study this process accurately.

Because the census records are organized by communities, and not by individuals, one particularly perplexing question remains unanswered at present. The evidence we have acquired so far suggests that people who arrived early in a community and prospered were prone to remain. The question that arises from this is whether those people who did not succeed and quickly moved on were able, by dint of early arrival in their next destination, to prosper there and so become permanent and well-established residents of that town. If not, then the prospect exists that the nineteenth century saw the development of a sizeable underclass of permanently mobile Americans who spent their lives searching for success and prosperity by moving from one place to another but never achieving their ultimate goal.

City directories, published yearly in some nineteenth-century communities by local governments or private agencies allow us to expand on some of the findings of persistence derived from the censuses. A series of directories listing the inhabitants of a particular community in successive years obviously eliminates many of the problems inherent in using censuses taken ten years apart. Not only do they provide evidence on persistence that can be used to explore whether individuals left after one, two, five, seven, or nine years, but they also can provide a much clearer documentation of the yearly amount of turnover within a particular community. An examination of the names on the first page of the *Schenectady City Directory* for 1865 and 1866, presented in Table VIII, shows a number of changes in just one year. Careful study also indicates that some of the residents who remained in Schenectady had moved within the town itself or had change their occupation. John Abel did both.

One extremely interesting study of Boston in the late nineteenth century, done from city directories by Stephan Thernstrom and Peter Knights, has demonstrated that, in spite of the fact that migration contributed only a small amount to Boston's growth over any ten-year period, there was an extraordinarily rapid movement of population into and out of the city. Thus, although on the surface Boston appeared to be a relatively stable community, compared to new urban areas like Chicago or Omaha, this appearance of stability was deceiving. Even in older eastern cities, population turned over so rapidly stability was not something that could be readily assured.

Sources that might be appropriately termed personal offer quite different perspectives on migrants and migration than the public records. Migrants often recorded their impressions of trips, either at the time via diaries or letters, or in memoirs written a number of years later. Frequently these impressions are highly subjective and are of uneven quality, but they are still of significant value to anyone who would understand the meaning of migration to individual human beings, and the details involved in moving from one place to another. Of course, many such personal recollections were written down in conjunction with a major move, such as a transatlantic voyage or crossing the great prairies in a covered wagon. A shorter move from one textile community to another within a particular state seldom called forth deliberate efforts to record the journey.

Personal records are tremendously important, both because they offer us insight into what it was like to spend several weeks on board a crowded ship or in a covered wagon crossing the prairies, and because they provide insight into the motives of the individual men and women who moved from one place to another. The ability to study the meaning of migration to individuals is especially valuable because one of the significant problems in any social science is to link the structures of society, and any changes in them, to personal experience and behavior. For example, it is often relatively easy to compare wage rates or shifts in occupational structures from one part of the world to another, and to set forth assumed reasons why any differences might have produced migration. Frequently, however, it is much more difficult to demonstrate that individual human beings actually responded to such structural changes in a conscious fashion. Of course, it was not always necessary for individuals to be aware of the general changes that were occurring in order for them to be uncomfortable in the particular place where they were living. Nonetheless, any ability we have to determine what particular individuals actually thought they were doing enhances our understanding of the process of migration immensely.

Careful use of personal documents can offer us interesting opportunities to distinguish what migration meant to particular ethnic groups or to males as opposed to females. Oscar Handlin has contributed significantly to our understanding of American history through his exploration of how various ethnic groups experienced the great transatlantic migrations in the nineteenth century. Comparable insights into the meaning of migration into the western United States have been made by John Modell in his studies of Japanese immigrants in the early twentieth century. John Faragher and Julie Jeffrey have made significant contributions to American history by demonstrating that moving west meant quite different things to women than to men in the nineteenth century. Faragher demonstrated that the Overland Trail, at least temporaily, altered patterns of behavior familiar to most women. Jeffrey was more concerned with how women responded to various environments once they were settled in the western territories, discovering among other things that they generally accepted the gender roles that were being defined for women living in more established and more urban environments.

Scholars who actually went out and interviewed migrants have provided similar insights into what it meant to be a mobile American. These studies have ranged over a wide variety of people. Clyde Kiser, for example, recorded the experiences of black Americans who left Georgia's Sea Islands and ultimately arrived in northern urban environments in the 1920s. Wilbur Shepperson explored what it meant to move to Nevada in the late nineteenth and early twentieth centuries, paying some attention to the experiences of men as opposed to women. Seattle business leaders and European intellectuals who moved to the United States in the 1930s are other groups who have been interviewed

Table VIII. City directories, Schenectady, N.Y., 1865 and 1866

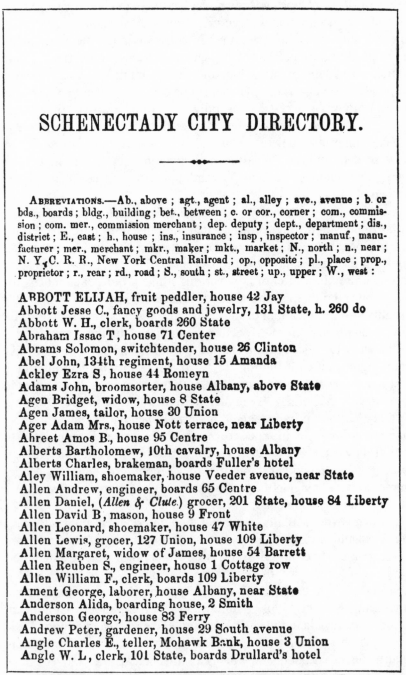

SCHENECTADY CITY DIRECTORY.

ABBREVIATIONS.—Ab., above ; agt., agent ; al., alley ; ave., avenue ; b. or bds., boards ; bldg., building ; bet., between ; c. or cor., corner ; com., commission ; com. mer., commission merchant ; dep. deputy ; dept., department ; dis., district ; E., east ; h., house ; ins., insurance ; insp , inspector ; manuf., manufacturer ; mer., merchant ; mkr., maker ; mkt., market ; N., north ; n., near ; N. Y. C. R. R., New York Central Railroad ; op., opposite ; pl., place ; prop., proprietor ; r., rear ; rd., road ; S., south ; st., street ; up., upper ; W., west :

ABBOTT ELIJAH, fruit peddler, house 42 Jay
Abbott Jesse C., fancy goods and jewelry, 131 State, h. 260 do
Abbott W. H., clerk, boards 260 State
Abraham Issac T, house 71 Center
Abrams Solomon, switchtender, house 26 Clinton
Abel John, 134th regiment, house 15 Amanda
Ackley Ezra S, house 44 Romeyn
Adams John, broomsorter, house Albany, above State
Agen Bridget, widow, house 8 State
Agen James, tailor, house 30 Union
Ager Adam Mrs., house Nott terrace, near Liberty
Ahreet Amos B., house 95 Centre
Alberts Bartholomew, 10th cavalry, house Albany
Alberts Charles, brakeman, boards Fuller's hotel
Aley William, shoemaker, house Veeder avenue, near State
Allen Andrew, engineer, boards 65 Centre
Allen Daniel, (*Allen & Clute*.) grocer, 201 State, house 84 Liberty
Allen David B, mason, house 9 Front
Allen Leonard, shoemaker, house 47 White
Allen Lewis, grocer, 127 Union, house 109 Liberty
Allen Margaret, widow of James, house 54 Barrett
Allen Reuben S., engineer, house 1 Cottage row
Allen William F., clerk, boards 109 Liberty
Ament George, laborer, house Albany, near State
Anderson Alida, boarding house, 2 Smith
Anderson George, house 83 Ferry
Andrew Peter, gardener, house 29 South avenue
Angle Charles E., teller, Mohawk Bank, house 3 Union
Angle W. L, clerk, 101 State, boards Drullard's hotel

STEINWAY & SONS', Gold Medal, Grand and Square Piano Fortes ; J. H. HIDLEY, 543 Broadway, sole Agent for Albany.

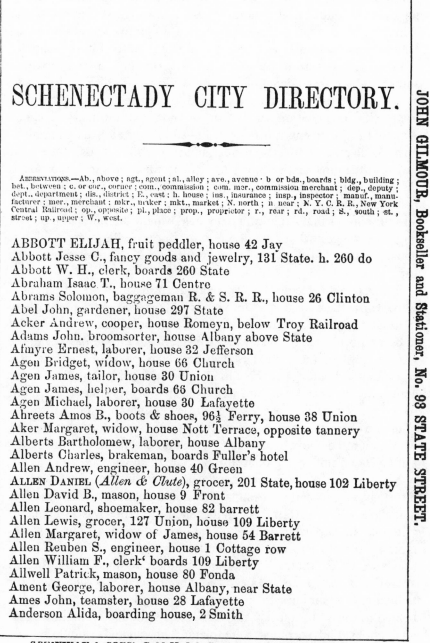

SCHENECTADY CITY DIRECTORY.

ABBREVIATIONS.—Ab., above ; agt., agent ; al., alley ; ave., avenue · b or bds., boards ; bldg., building ; bet., between ; c. or cor., corner ; com., commission ; com. mer., commission merchant ; dep., deputy ; dept., department ; dis., district ; E., east ; h. house ; ins., insurance ; insp., inspector ; manuf., manufacturer ; mer., merchant ; mkr., maker ; mkt., market ; N. north ; n. near ; N. Y. C. R. R., New York Central Railroad ; op., opposite ; pl., place ; prop., proprietor ; r., rear ; rd., road ; S., south ; st., street ; up., upper ; W., west.

ABBOTT ELIJAH, fruit peddler, house 42 Jay
Abbott Jesse C., fancy goods and jewelry, 131 State. h. 260 do
Abbott W. H., clerk, boards 260 State
Abraham Isaac T., house 71 Centre
Abrams Solomon, baggageman R. & S. R. R., house 26 Clinton
Abel John, gardener, house 297 State
Acker Andrew, cooper, house Romeyn, below Troy Railroad
Adams John. broomsorter, house Albany above State
Afmyre Ernest, laborer, house 32 Jefferson
Agen Bridget, widow, house 66 Church
Agen James, tailor, house 30 Union
Agen James, helper, boards 66 Church
Agen Michael, laborer, house 30 Lafayette
Ahreets Amos B., boots & shoes, 96½ Ferry, house 38 Union
Aker Margaret, widow, house Nott Terrace, opposite tannery
Alberts Bartholomew, laborer, house Albany
Alberts Charles, brakeman, boards Fuller's hotel
Allen Andrew, engineer, house 40 Green
ALLEN DANIEL (*Allen & Clute*), grocer, 201 State, house 102 Liberty
Allen David B., mason, house 9 Front
Allen Leonard, shoemaker, house 82 barrett
Allen Lewis, grocer, 127 Union, house 109 Liberty
Allen Margaret, widow of James, house 54 Barrett
Allen Reuben S., engineer, house 1 Cottage row
Allen William F., clerk' boards 109 Liberty
Allwell Patrick, mason, house 80 Fonda
Ament George, laborer, house Albany, near State
Ames John, teamster, house 28 Lafayette
Anderson Alida, boarding house, 2 Smith

JOHN GILMOUR, Bookseller and Stationer, No. 98 STATE STREET.

STEINWAY & SONS', Gold Medal, Grand and Square Piano Fortes; J. H. HIDLEY, 543 Broadway, sole Agent for Albany.

SOURCE: Schenectady City Directories on file in Schaffer Library, Union College, Schenectady, N.Y.

to see how and why they settled where they did. Such studies are of considerable value, but obviously are more difficult to replicate as the migrants age and die. The value of these works suggests, however, that it might now be worth interviewing recent migrants within and to the United States, in order to have comparable data for future analysis.

In between governmental and personal records are a wide variety of sources of use to students of migration. Some are directly linked to migration; others are not as clearly tied to the process, yet, if they are used with imagination, they can provide extraordinary insights. Among the documents most closely linked to migration are pamphlets, posters, fliers, and advertisements published by railroads, states, and towns in the nineteenth century to attract individuals to new lands in the West. Because these documents were designed to lure people to particular regions where land was available, they provided evidence into the appeals that Americans felt would win the attention of potential migrants, suggest what kind of economic opportunities were available, and indicate what modes of transportation were present to ease the trip.

By the late nineteenth century, recruitment by railroads of potential European settlers for midwestern lands had evolved to the point where railroad companies offered immigrants transportation across Europe to ocean ports, passage on a vessel to America, railroad passage to the western part of the United States, and land or a job in their new community. Under such conditions, the intervening obstacles that confronted a possible migrant were considerably less than those faced by migrants in earlier decades or centuries. Similar assistance also was offered to Mormon converts in various parts of northwestern Europe who sought to move from their homeland to the new Zion of the Latter Day Saints being built around Salt Lake City.

Nineteenth-century immigrants who were interested in seeking information about their destinations could refer to a vast body of guidebooks and travelers' accounts. Such literature was available to migrants in earlier periods, but not as extensively. These works typically offered information about what various parts of the United States were like, about various transportation options for traveling to and within the United States, and about what was necessary for individuals or families to take with them and what should be left behind to make the journey as comfortable as possible. Some of these guidebooks and accounts were blatant propaganda, published by investors in particular regions; other authors were more neutral about the territory they were describing.

These documents are especially important because they allow us to look at the prospect of immigration from the point of view of the men and women who were deciding whether or not to move. It was this material that provided them with their expectations about what migration would mean; knowledge gained during the actual trip was of little use. Once they were involved in the trip, they might find their chosen guidebook was extremely accurate or highly misleading, but by then it was too late to change their minds. Only by understanding the information that migrants had available to them can we assess many of their decisions about why and where they went. Clearly, objective assessments about migrants' destinations are desireable, but it is important to put such assessments in the context of the information available to the migrants themselves. Curiously, these guidebooks and travelers' accounts are much more common for agricultural regions in the western part of the United States than they are for the eastern urban areas. This is ironic because the different rhythms of life demanded in an urban industrial environment may have made a good guidebook far more desirable in those circumstances than it would have been for an agricultural community.

In recent years a number of scholars, particularly cultural geographers, have realized that the remnants of material culture from the past can be used effectively to determine migration patterns and the effects of those patterns on particular communities. We will comment more extensively on the results of some of these studies shortly, but they deserve brief mention here since they rely on unusual and often overlooked sources. Because different groups of people tend to respond to particular environments according to their cultural predispositions, careful observation of such things as the layout of the fields, where and how roads are built, town patterns, placement of farm houses, house types, fencing, layout of cemetaries, the kinds of crops that are grown, and even the names that are given to particular geographic features can be used to trace the flow of migrants across the land. An observant traveler may still today see evidence of old roads, bridges, trails, and canals that shaped the direction of migration in earlier periods. Similarly, houses, steeples, crops, and town organization can suggest to the keen eye the origins of the individuals who settled a particular region. Where maps exist over a long period of time, they, too, can shed insight into the evolution of local communities, and suggest how neighboring communities may have differed one from another.

Interdisciplinary Perspectives on Migration

Examination so far of the history, theories, and sources involved in studying migration should make it clear that extensive interdisciplinary cooperation and training are necessary if the subject is to be fully understood. Because several of the more traditional and better known topics of migration in American history have been touched on in conjunction with our discussion above, the remainder of the chapter will focus on five relatively new and unfamiliar aspects of the subject, in order to demonstrate some of the more interesting findings that interdisciplinary work has produced in recent years. The works of Maldwyn Jones and Philip Taylor, listed in the suggested readings for this chapter, offer excellent syntheses for many of the more traditional lines of study, especially regarding international migration. The first three topics reflect some of the extraordinary contributions geographers have made to our understanding of migration. A look at Americans' relationship to both their land and water will show the vital role those relationships have played in American history. Then, this section will explore how transportation has shaped the American past, with special emphasis on how American urban communities have developed. The use of language and how it shapes our understanding of migration is a topic that commands attention, both in terms of how migrants themselves used words, and how students of migration have written about the subject. Finally, it is of interest to ask whether students can sensibly study American history or only the history of Americans as a collection of different peoples.

1. Land and People

Throughout much of American history, agriculture has been the main source of income for most people. Therefore, it is interesting to ask how Americans chose the land on which they eventually settled, how they acquired it, and how they used the land. In exploring these questions, the wide range of disciplines involved in studying migration can be demonstrated.

Choosing the land was an important process involving a complex chain of information and evaluation. Migrants carefully selected particular types of land for various reasons that ultimately directed certain kinds of people to one region of the United States and other groups elsewhere. One of the most common elements that went into choosing the land was simply that it looked like home. Thus, Finns who moved to the United States in the nineteenth century chose to settle in parts of Minnesota that reminded them of the land they had left instead of on the Kansas prairies. Likewise, Cherokee Indians, who were forced out of western Georgia in the 1830s, ultimately settled in parts of the Ozarks in Arkansas and Oklahoma that were similar to the mountains they had left involuntarily. West Virginians left mountainous regions in the eastern part of the United States and trekked all the way across the prairies and plains to settle in familiar environments in the mountain valleys of Oregon.

A second element migrants considered when deciding where to settle was the character of the people already there. Ethnic ghettos developed in rural areas, as people preferred to take up residence near neighbors with common values. This process worked to separate English from Polish immigrants in a single Wisconsin county, or it might occur on a broader scale. Migrants to Utah had particular religious preferences; those who chose to go to California after the gold rush had an orientation toward adventure and mining; settlers who moved to Oregon generally were interested in establishing small farms, first in the Willamette Valley, and then farther east in the more open spaces of the Oregon prairies. The struggles between slaveholders and free soil advocates in the 1850s over the settlement of Kansas indicates clearly that Americans understood how the first group to dominate a particular region shaped the evolution of that town, county, or state in the years that followed.

Every ethnic group had its own ideas regarding what constituted good soil and how much timber was needed on a farm that they used to evaluate and determine which regions were preferable and which should be passed over. Finn's, for example, rejected the relatively open lands of Illinois and Iowa to settle in the forest and lake regions of Minnesota that reminded them of home. Sometimes migrants made their decisions using guidebooks that described territories with varying degrees of accuracy, but often individuals or groups depended on their own immediate observation of lands and environments as they worked their way west. Soil types were particularly important to many immigrants in search of new and potentially prosperous farm land. Sometimes accurately and sometimes not, farmers in the nineteenth century associated sandy soils, clays, dark soils, or light soils with the possibility of growing particular kinds of crops for which they had preferences. In addition, their heritage led them to believe that certain kinds of soils would be much easier to work with the agricultural implements of the nineteenth century than other kinds. Thus, in a state like Missouri, immigrants from Germany were often on the lookout for soils that would allow them to grow potatoes or fruit crops, while settlers with a English background, perhaps from older regions in the South, showed an interest in lands that could be used to grow cotton.

Scholars have long debated how nineteenth-century agriculturalists used the presence or absence of timber in evaluating the potential of farmland. Initially it was argued that nineteenth-century migrants frequently believed the absence of timber was evidence of soil that was not particularly fertile. More recent studies by geographers such as Terry Jordan have indicated that nineteenth-century farmers were in fact more sophisticated than that. They recognized that open lands were actually quite desirable because they did not require clearing before they could be used for farming, and they understood as well that open prairies could be extraordinarily fertile, though sometimes such land needed to be drained before it could be used. An absence of trees often indicated swampy areas in which timber simply does not grow well. The reluctance of farmers to settle far from timber was based on other, very practical considerations throughout much of the first three-quarters of the nineteenth century. Wood was necessary for housing, for fuel during the long, cold winter months in the central part of the United States, and for fences. By the end of the nineteenth century, coal mining and barbed wire helped to free farmers from their dependence on timber for heat and fencing, but they still needed wood for housing. However, by 1875, lumber could be imported for the one-time construction of a house from a considerable distance.

To understand the decisions that migrants made in selecting their lands it is also necessary to know something about climate in the nineteenth century, in terms of both the historical evolution of climates and the yearly cycles that characterized particular regions. It is also important to understand what ideas migrants had about climate. Perhaps no region in America that was subject to European agricultural practices in the nineteenth century has been discussed as often as in as varied terms with regard to climate as the territory between the one-hundredth meridian and the Rocky Mountains. Both nineteenth-century Americans and their twentieth-century chroniclers have described this land as a desert and a garden. Surely it is difficult to envision two more divergent images.

The question is how and why two such contrasting images could be used to describe the same region. Recent research suggests several plausible answers. To begin, in the middle of the nineteenth century, a three-hundred-year-long cycle in world climate seems to have come to an end, bringing gradual but significant changes in temperature and rainfall to various parts of the northern hemisphere. In addition, the interior of the United States has, since at least 1850, experienced twenty-year cycles of dry and wet weather. Thus, guidebooks or travelers' accounts describing this territory either as a desert or a garden may accurately reflect the conditions of the year in which the observations were made. An additional source of confusion about this territory depends on when the observers actually passed through the region. In early May, this land can appear quite verdent and luxurious, particularly if one is coming from the drier parts of Texas, but by August the territory can look quite brown and bleak, especially if one has recently passed through the moister, greener parts of Wisconsin or Iowa.

Clearly, understanding the decisions of nineteenth-century migrants about the desirability of a particular location requires not only a current evaluation of the climate of that region, but also some sensitivity to what the climate may have been like in various decades in the past, as well as the yearly cycles of temperature and rainfall in different parts of the United States. Decisions that may appear irrational today may have been sensible, given the observations migrants made when they were present in a region.

Other attitudes about climate were important in shaping nineteenth- and early twentieth-century patterns of migration. Some nineteenth-century Americans believed that human habitation could actually change climate for the better. The adage that was frequently used was that rain follows the plow—the land, when it was turned over and opened up for agriculture, would, by some ill-defined process, produce the rain required to allow crops to grow. What appeared to be empirical evidence for this belief may have been produced by short-term climate cycles. But the long-term results of acting on this idea often were disastrous. The Dust Bowl that developed in Oklahoma and continued north into the Dakotas in the 1930s was the most notable product of this attitude. When this territory was initially opened up for agriculture, rainfall was adequate for the crops that were to be grown there. But in the 1930s, the climate cycle produced several years of inadequate crops and severe erosion of the soil by wind. Clearly, rain had not followed the plow but had been present because of short-term climate cycles.

Occasionally a migrant's choice of destination involved evaluations regarding climate, environment, and possible benefits to health. Some regions were avoided in the nineteenth century because of climate that appeared conducive to sundry ill-defined illnesses. Frequently these decisions made considerable sense, at least with regard to the upper Mississippi River Valley and the Missouri River Valley where malaria was common during much of the middle part of the nineteenth century. Other states attracted people because they acquired a reputation for providing good health. Florida, Minnesota, Arizona, and southern California are among regions in the United States where individuals moved in the nineteenth century in search of better health and a longer life. Certain kinds of illnesses, such as tuberculosis, actually may have subsided in these new and more healthful environments, though for reasons that would not have been understood at the time.

Choosing the land was only the first step in establishing a new residence. Once a migrant decided that a particular region was attractive, it was necessary to acquire a suitable plot of land. In order to fully comprehend the process by which land was transferred from public to private hands, it is necessary to understand politics, surveying, and finance. Politics is important on two levels. First, the government of the United States had to acquire territories west of the Mississippi by war or treaty. Sometimes this history, which is essentially diplomatic and political in its orientation, involves the relationship of the United States with European governments or Mexico, but it also includes the often overlooked story of the Indians' retreat westward, and their ultimate isolation on reservations, on land that in the nineteenth century was considered extremely undesirable. One of the ironies of American history is that in the twentieth century it was discovered that many Indian reservations included some of the most important mineral reserves in the western parts of the United States.

Any student of western migration ultimately needs to know something about land law and custom. On one level this can inform the sophisticated observer about who settled a particular territory. Cultural differences in how land was to be divided and fields laid out are reflected in maps and aerial photos, and can be used to determine who settled in a particular territory. Patterns of land distribution in the English colonies were remarkably different from those where the French or Spanish first settled. Figure 9 presents an interesting example from Missouri where Spanish land grants laid out with some attention to the terrain was partly divided into the long, narrow fields common in French agricultural settlements, and was later surrounded by the rectangular land grants oriented to the compass that characterized American traditions after 1785. From evidence like this, it is possible to demonstrate the sequence of political domination in the Mississippi River Valley and to reflect on the attitudes about land, farming, and even community life that are inherent in the size and shape of fields.

Figure 9. Land claims and cultural preferences in Washington County, Missouri.

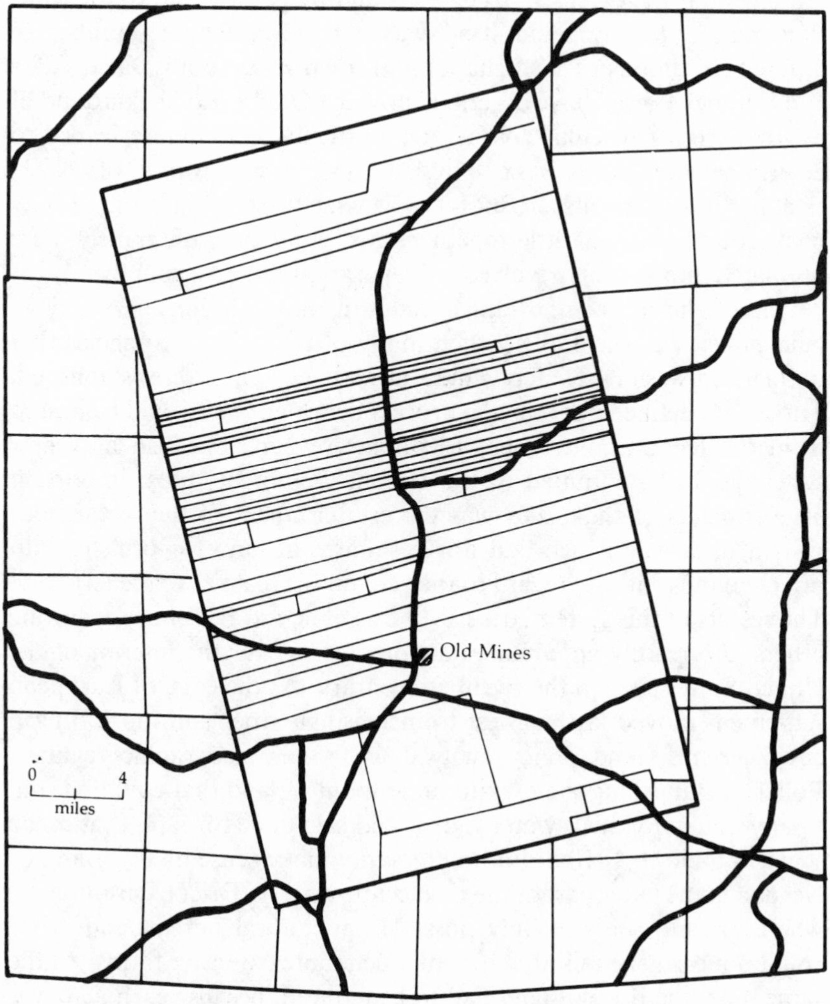

SOURCE: Reprinted from *Immigrants in the Ozarks: A Study in Ethnic Geography* by Russel L. Gerlach by permission of the University of Missouri Press. Copyright 1976 by the Curators of the University of Missouri.

Even within the territories dominated by the English, landholding patterns were not always the same. New England, in the seventeenth century, was dominated by close-knit villages and fields surrounding those communities, while a more scattered pattern of settlement evolved in Virginia. Stilgoe has recently commented on these and other aspects of landscape common before 1845. Part of this simply reflects differences in the New World environment; because the hills and valleys of New England were not as conducive to widespread settlement as the extensive waterways and flat land of the Chesapeake Bay region. But England itself was a country with a number of different traditions of field shapes and town plots. Both David Allen and Sumner Powell have described how the Old World background of migrants to a particular colony or a particular community helped to determine the most basic physical and social forms of newly established settlements. In Sudbury, Massachusetts, men from distinct background tried to settle together, but found their differences were ultimately more easily resolved by separation than by compromise.

One of the most important decades in the evolution of American land policy was the 1780s, when many of the laws and policies that ultimately transferred federal lands into private hands were established. These laws defined not only the process by which land would be passed from the federal government to private owners, but also how new states would be admitted to the Union. One of the most important developments of the 1780s was the establishment of the rectangular system of survey which laid down squares of land for transfer into private hands without regard to the geographic realities of the territory. The results of this system, described by Hildegard B. Johnson, among others, are readily apparent to anyone flying over the interior of the United States even in the twentieth century. As the edge of European settlement moved farther west to increasingly drier and more rugged environments, land policy evolved to fit new geographic realities. Policies establishing the maximum amount of land that could be sold to any one individual, water rights, and sale price for land that made sense in Ohio in 1810 did not necessarily make sense in Wyoming or Nevada in the latter part of the nineteenth century. Drier environments, where grazing was the only possible agricultural pursuit and crops could not easily be raised, required much more extensive farms. At the same time, the price of land had to be reduced, because each acre was intrinsically less valuable in the Far West than it was in the eastern parts of the United States. Access to waterways had to be more carefully guaranteed where rainfall was scarce.

Financing the purchase of land is also an important element in the story of migration. It was only after 1863 that Americans could acquire farm land from the federal government by means of establishing a homestead and living on a plot of land for a minimum number of years. Prior to that time, and most commonly after 1863 as well, farmers bought land, occasionally from the federal government, but more often from speculators who had acquired large chunks of land from national or state governments. Railroad companies, which acquired significant amounts of territory west of the Mississippi as inducements to building the transcontinental railroads in the mid-nineteenth century, played an important element in opening up the western part of the United States. Single speculators or groups of investors commonly purchased large amounts of land with the intent of selling smaller plots to farmers. The financial histories of the successes and failures of speculators is often fascinating. It is necessary, however, to avoid the older interpretation of American history that portrayed speculators in opposition to farmers in their basic interests, because many farmers were themselves speculators on a more modest level. Many farmers moved into a relatively unsettled territory, cleared and plowed the land, built houses, barns, and fences, and ultimately sold the farm to someone else and moved on. Some speculators operated on a larger scale than others, but speculation in land values has been a common element in American history from the seventeenth century to the present.

The cultural heritage of migrants was often as important as the physical realities of the environment in determining how the land was used once it had been acquired. Obviously, environment played some role in shaping agricultural choices within a particular region. It is simply impossible to grow crops such as rice in large parts of the interior of the United States. There is too little rainfall and the temperatures are much too cold. Lands lying east of the one-hundredth meridian generally were appropriate for plowing and growing crops; in contrast, drier regions to the west could only be used for grazing. Even these divisions require further elaboration, because in some territories cattle could graze but in others only sheep might easily survive. However, in particular dry regions, sheep, which crop grass extremely close to the soil, could be dangerous in terms of the long-term fertility by increasing the probability of erosion. Similarly, in some regions farmers could choose from a wide selection of crops, ranging from fruits to potatoes, cotton, or grains. Elsewhere, choices were more limited.

In spite of the importance of physical limits, scholars have demonstrated that, from the seventeenth century to the present, the layout of fields and the choice of crops, phenomena that are basic to the daily and yearly rhythms of life that a farmer and his family experience, were at least partially determined by ethnic background. It is easy to overlook how important these fundamental decisions were in shaping not only daily rhythms of life, but in some instances, major political problems as well. One of the very first sources of trouble between the English and the Indians emerged from the fact that the English preferred to fence in their fields and let their animals roam loose, foraging where they might. The fact that these animals frequently foraged in the unfenced Indian grain fields caused considerable friction. Eighteenth-century German migrants generally paid much more attention to providing sound barns for stroing their crops and protecting their animals, and more often preferred to grow rootcrops and fruits, than did their British counterparts. Curiously, exactly the same kinds of contrasts existed in Alabama in 1929. Alabama farmers of German background made choices similar to those made by their counterparts in Pennsylvania 150 years earlier, whereas farmers with British ethnic roots continued to practice agriculture much as their ancestors did in Pennsylvania a century and a half before, except for the fact that cotton replaced grain in the deep South. One particularly interesting example of how cultures and environment interact is the examination by Evon Vogt and Ethel Albert of the community they referred to as Rimrock in eastern New Mexico where Texans, Mormons, Hispanic Americans, Navajos, and Zuni Indians all shared a common environment. However, each of these groups practiced somewhat different forms of agriculture, and demonstrated different attitudes towards the land as well.

2. Water

Consideration of the importance of land in the study of migration in American history leads naturally to the topic of water. This is a subject that deserves much fuller attention than it has received in the past. In the twentieth century, much of our concern is obviously with regard to dry lands. As Americans increasingly move into the Sun Belt, especially into the southwestern parts of the United States where water is scarce, they must find water for irrigation and for desert cities that are developing in climates not well suited to extensive human habitation. Thus, our recent history emphasizes water shortages and the need to transport water over long distances. This requires an understanding not only of water law, but also of the technology of water storage and transport. It might be argued that the history of Los Angeles has been shaped far more by the city's long-term capabilities to acquire the water necessary to allow relatively unimpeded growth than by an initial decision by a railroad to favor that community.

Ironically, in the middle of the nineteenth century, too much water was often a more serious problem facing migrants than too little water. Much of the land drained by the Mississippi River and its contributers was wet rather than dry. Swamps threatened not only health but also the ability of farmers to plow lands and grow crops. In fact, rather large-scale drainage projects in Ohio, Indiana, Illinois, and Iowa were necessary before many of these lands were effectively open to full-scale agricultural exploitation. It has been argued that more land in the United States had to be drained to make it accessible to farmers than has had to be irrigated.

Water has also served both to unify particular parts of the country and to divide one section of the United States from another. In the era when transportation was dominated by ocean, river, and canal traffic, water frequently served to unify particular regions. Both Massachusetts Bay and the Chesapeake Bay became cores of a common way of life. Similarly, the Mississippi River Valley or the Willamette Valley in Oregon became a closely integrated economic unit because of the river flowing through there. In the early parts of the nineteenth century canals were also important in tying regions together. The development of upstate New York clearly hinged on the Erie Canal even though early settlements in western New York, Ohio, and Indiana had been established before the Canal had been completely dug. Later, as land transportation became more important, water could provide a dividing force as railroads and later highways had to find their way around, over, or under large bodies of water.

3. Cities and Transportation

Because many nineteenth-century Americans chose to go to cities rather than agricultural frontiers, it is worth asking how cities came to be located where they were and what led people to choose to move to them. Any exploration of this subject naturally is involved in a consideration of transportation changes in the nineteenth century. It is important to remember that American history in general and the history of American migration in particular are very closely tied to two of the great transportation revolutions in world history—namely the extraordinary improvements in navigational skills and implements and in the construction of ocean-going and river-going vessels that occurred between the fifteenth and nineteenth centuries, and the equally extraordinary development in continental transportation between the eighteenth and twentieth centuries involving first canals, then railroads, and ultimately highways.

The interaction of immigrant experience, transportation, and urban biography is clearly visible in studies that explore how the foreign born of particular origins came to be concentrated in particular cities and what those concentrations meant to the cities involved, whether the people under study are the Dutch who settled in Kalamazoo, Michigan, the Irish who came to dominate Boston, Massachusetts, or Italians and Poles who settled in Chicago, Illinois. The location of a particular ethnic group in a given city was often the unintended consequence of decisions regarding transportation routes. For example, many Irish ended up in Boston simply because British mailboats traveled from England to Boston, and then sent their mail overland into Canada. The Irish took the most convenient transportation to North America, and ended up in Boston. Similarly, many Germans arrived in cities in the Mississippi River Valley such as St. Louis, New Orleans, or Cincinnati, or in urban communities in Texas, because the vessels on which they crossed the Atlantic docked first in New Orleans. The reasons why immigrants from China, Japan, or the Philippines entered the United States through Pacific coast ports are also very obvious.

Such observations only touch the surface of the complex process by which cities became the places where the majority of Americans live. Most urban migrants, whether from abroad or from within the United States, came to communities that were already established. Hence, it is important to ask why cities grew where they did. With the exception of Washington, D.C., the location of the most dominant American cities has been profoundly affected by large-scale geographic features; many smaller cities reflect the additional influences of regional economies and speculation by individuals or corporations. Large-scale geographic influences worked primarily in conjunction with developing transportation networks. Urban places emerged where routes naturally crossed or where changes in the forms of transportation were necessary.

The great ports of the United States, Boston, New York, New Orleans, and San Francisco, are obvious examples of the links between transportation, geography, and population growth. Albany in upstate New York, Chicago, Illinois, Atlanta, Georgia, and Louisville, Kentucky, grew for similar reasons. Albany, for example, dominates the intersection of the Hudson-Champlain corridor north and south and the east-west route that starts with the Mohawk River Valley, and extends westward through the Finger Lakes, to the Great Lakes in the interior of the northern part of the North American continent. Chicago is located at the tip of Lake Michigan, a very convenient point where land and water travel come together. Anyone moving westward who wished to go into the northern plains states ultimately had to circle around the Great Lakes and pass the tip of Lake Michigan in the Chicago region. Atlanta is a dryland equivalent to Chicago. Atlanta's location, near the southern tip of the Appalachian Mountain chain, is one of the convenient locations where travelers moving north and south along the mountains could first turn and go east to west. Louisville grew at the point on the Ohio River where the falls required early river boats to unload their goods and people, which then had to be moved overland before being reloaded on the other side of the falls.

Obviously, a large-scale geographic feature such as the Appalachian Mountain chain or the Great Lakes offers a certain amount of choice regarding the exact location of a major urban center. Perth Amboy is one of the first urban areas that failed in its competition with what is now a major city, in this case New York City, to dominate a particular harbor. The New Jersey rival was the victim of human choices regarding where the urban center was to develop at the mouth of the Hudson. Similarly, Kansas City, Houston, and Los Angeles were involved in the early years of their development in intense rivalries with neighboring communities, and were successful because they attracted the interests of speculators, particularly railroad speculators, rather than because of any intrinsically advantageous local geographic factor. Manhattan Island or Philadelphia did not need to dominate the Hudson River Valley or the Delaware River Valley respectively, but if they had not some other city would have likely emerged in the vicinity.

Geographers and economists have shown us how once major cities did emerge in various parts of the country, then regional economies also developed with hierarchies of urban places. The central city that provided many basic functions for a regional economy often times had smaller communities in its orbit, and these towns in turn had their own satellites. Frequently these smaller communities decreased in size according to quite regular population ratios. Transportation networks were tied closely to networks of economic activity, exchange of information, and patterns of population distribution and growth.

Over long periods of time, initial patterns of regional settlement are subject to change in response to new transportation technology and increasing speed of communication. Faster transmission of information and goods enables large towns to extend their influence farther and farther afield, bringing once dominant regional centers into their hierarchies and reducing them to sattelite towns. This, in turn, can change population distribution, though not always in the same way.

East of the Mississippi, technological changes in transportation in the nineteenth century were introduced into a context of already established communities so that railroads were built from one existing town to another, frequently in the midst of considerable urban rivalry. West of the Mississippi, where settlement and technological change in transportation occurred at the same time, decisions about where railroads would send their lines were much more closely connected to both the initial and long-term growth of an eventual urban center.

Transportation networks within particular communities and the ensuing patterns of population distribution are as fascinating as the evolution of transportation networks between communities and regions. Early towns, such as New York and Boston, grew by rather ill-defined processes in the seventeenth century whereby individuals followed preexisting trails, natural landforms, and the whimsy of private choice in laying out roads and establishing residences. In 1683, William Penn was successful in imposing a rather carefully planned grid design on Philadelphia. As John Reps has shown in his careful and fascinating studies of town planning in America, Penn's plan was one of the most influential in American urban history. Many of our largest cities adopted a grid pattern in response to the early evolution and advantage that Philadelphia found to streets laid out at right angles. Although rigid attention to geometrical forms does not always make a great deal of sense in terms of local land forms, it does provide a rational process by which individuals can locate themselves within a city and find any particular street address. In addition, Americans who frequently moved from one community to another found it easy to adapt to their new location.

Railroad technology affected the evolution of large American cities in the nineteenth century not only by opening up large hinterlands to these vast metropolises but also through the creation of rail networks that provided urban communities with more rapid short-distance travel. Before streetcars, subways, and commuter railroads were available, cities could only be as large as was possible for a person to walk across and back in one day. Thus, "walking" cities were relatively small and congested, with residential neighborhoods overlapping industrial and commercial zones because people had to live near where they worked. Frequently, the more prosperous residents of cities lived in the center of town, while their poorer neighbors resided some distance from commercial and industrial areas where they daily confronted the long walk to and from work. As streetcar systems, local railroad networks, and subways were built, suburbs began to grow because people could live some distance from their work. This produced not only growth in the urban area but also a new pattern of residential arrangements whereby more prosperous urban residents could remove themselves from the hustle and bustle, the noise, and smells of the central city to a more tranquil environment on the metropolitan fringes.

The evolution of transportation patterns within local communities were often quite different. Schenectady, New York, grew in response to a succession of a least three major transportation systems. The community initially was established at a bend in the Mohawk River, and streets ran parallel and perpendicular to the river for several blocks inland. In the early part of the nineteenth century, two major transportation changes caused the reorientation of the community, though a major fire in 1819 made this reorientation easier than it might have been. To begin, the construction of the Erie Canal, running parallel to the river but several blocks inland, moved the major business sections away from the edge of the river to streets bordering the canal. Several years later, in the early 1830s, the completion of a railroad link between Albany and Schenectady that ended on a hilltop above and to the east of the canal and river plain introduced an east-west influence into Schenectady building that reduced the importance of the streets running north and south parallel to the river and the canal.

In Chicago, a satisfactory transportation system depended on two major changes. First, a low, swampy location required the whole town to raise the level of its streets and to jack up its buildings to the new street level. In addition, after the great Chicago fire, the main streets of the town were reoriented from east and west to north and south along Lake Michigan as the result of decisions by powerful local merchants and real estate investors. Los Angeles, a more recent American community, is a city with no real center, partly because it grew as a collection of suburbs linked by local railroads, and this pattern was enhanced by automobile traffic and freeways. Historians need to explore more fully the influence of the interstate highway system, not only on the distribution of population in the United States, but also on the recent evolution of urban areas and their suburbs.

Because of the importance of the automobile in shaping the local, regional, and national distribution of population in the twentieth century, historians need to pay more attention to the history of the building of highways. A few studies of roads in the history of the nation suggest the importance of this topic. From the early years of the republic to the present, there has been an ongoing debate about whether national, state, or local governments should be responsible for the building and maintenance of our highway system. Until the end of the nineteenth century, roads often were primitive and poorly kept. Major efforts to improve roads emerged late in the nineteenth century, partly as a result of the bicycle craze, but more importantly as part of the efforts of rural areas to achieve easier access to urban communities. As automobiles became a more important part of American society, the demand for better roads became irresistible.

The building of hard-surfaced, all-weather roads has changed land values, shifted population concentrations, and even determined the number and kind of animals present in rural areas. All of these subjects have been studied in some detail by historians in a few local communities, but it would be helpful for us to know more about the effects of all-weather roads elsewhere. The fact that better highways in Nebraska reduced the number of horses used for travel in rural areas and therefore made available lands for commercial crops once needed for hay may be important to Nebraska's history, but it does not necessarily tell us what happened in similar situations in Wisconsin, Ohio, New York, or California.

4. Language and Migration

An often overlooked aspect of migration is an awareness of how language was used by migrants and those who have sought to portray their experience. Studies of language can range from meanings of particular words to the myths and values associated with migration. They can increase our understanding of what migration meant to people, what motivated them, and how individuals experienced the broad structural patterns that can be described from government documents. We have already commented on the letters, diaries, and memoirs in which men and women recorded their experience with journeys as varied as those from Europe to the United States, or from Missouri to a destination in Texas, Utah, Oregon, or California. However, there are at least two other aspects of language that deserve note.

Language has played a critical role in encouraging the expansion of white Americans westward across the continent. From William Bradford's seventeenth-century history of the Plymouth Plantation, in which he described Cape Cod as being a, "hideous and desolate wilderness, full of wild beasts and wild men," to nineteenth-century discussions of America's "manifest destiny," in which the population was portrayed as rolling like an irresistible wave across North America until it reached the Pacific, a language of conquest has been common in American society. This language has made expropriation of lands held by other people perhaps easier than it otherwise would have been.

Books written in the nineteenth century and by twentieth-century historians frequently are full of remarks on empty space and free land. One student of 1845 Swiss migrants to Wisconsin describes a passage by one of the early settlers, in which the pioneer noted the lighting of the first fire, the eating of the first food, and the catching of the first fish in the local brook. The historian comments on the irony of recording this rather impressive list of "firsts," in view of the fact that the author also mentioned the presence of an Indian village on the land on which he and his friends were already encroaching. This is only one example of the remarkable ability of Europeans moving to America to view American land as empty, even though it was in fact occupied. What Europeans failed to realize or admit was that space not utilized according to Old World agricultural traditions was not necessarily empty.

Similarly, discussions of free land in American history are equally inappropriate, whether "free land" is used to refer to land unoccupied by other human inhabitants, or is taken in a more limited financial sense to refer to land that could be acquired by farmers at no cost. Throughout almost all of American history the land was rarely free in either sense of the word. Francis Jennings has made a major contribution to our understanding of the resettlement process through his observation that the most appropriate metaphor to describe North America was a widowed rather than a virgin land. Some have suggested that whether virgin or widowed, the land was soon ravished by white males.

Although the question probably can never be unequivocally answered, it is worth asking whether different choices of words might have made it more difficult for Europeans to expand across North America. Reference to a frontier, generally perceived as a boundary separating civilization from savagery, surely made it easier for Europeans to seize the land of those they felt to be savage, and hence incapable of using the land as God had intended. Geographers have tried to use more neutral terms in current studies of the expansion of European areas of settlement. For example, rather than writing about frontiers, geographers frequently refer to borderlands or zones of contact between cultures, implying not superior civilization on one side and inferior on the other, but rather that cultures of equal worth, but of different style and organization, could be found in the midst of and extending away from a particular zone of contact. With this kind of language, there is no inherent judgment that one group had the right to expand into the other's territory.

Another approach to migration through language that has yet to receive the attention that it perhaps deserves is an examination of how novelists have portrayed the experience of migrants. Comparison of the actual historical record to the work of novelists who have chosen migration as their subject demonstrates that novelists frequently have portrayed quite accurately and effectively much of what it meant to be a mobile American. In fact, novelists' freedom to create situations and dialogue enables them to communicate in a single work what historians can only achieve through more extensive, specialized, and limited studies.

Three novels of the move westward indicate the value of this literature, both as a supplement to history and, in some cases, as part of the record of those who lived at the time. O. E. Rolvaag, in his two remarkable novels on Norwegian experiences on the great plains, *Giants in the Earth* and *Peder Victorious,* has been sensitive to a number of important issues that can be historically documented. One of the main themes in *Giants in the Earth* is the sharp difference between the perceptions and reactions of men and women to life in an isolated, underdeveloped region. Rolvaag's men welcomed the adventure and new opportunity that the North American plains offered to them. The women, on the other hand, often feared the primitive, unfamiliar land as a place in which family and cultural traditions were dangerously threatened. The story includes instances of women who were driven to the borderlines of insanity and beyond.

In *Peder Victorious,* Rolvaag's sequel to his first extraordinary novel, Rolvaag develops three additional themes about the migrant's experience. He demonstrates that eventually women did accommodate themselves, sometimes quite successfully, to the new North American environment. However, he also shows that living in the United States produced a significant conflict between the original generation who left Europe and their children who were born in America, and so had no direct ties with the old country. According to Rolvaag, one of the most disturbing experiences an immigrant family could confront was the possibility of a marriage between one of their own children and a child of a quite different culture. The mother in *Peder Victorious,* who was portrayed in the first novel as driven to dispair by the loneliness of the prairies, becomes equally distraught over the prospect of her

Norwegian Lutheran son marrying the daughter of a neighboring Irish Catholic family. This is especially interesting because scholars recently have begun to explore interethnic and interracial marriages as measures of cultural assimilation on the part of immigrants. Here is a rather pointed instance of a novelist anticipating a theme that historians are only now emphasizing as an important way to study the immigrant experience.

Owen Wister's *The Virginian* has achieved considerable fame as the model for a whole genre of American literature—the western. Yet in reading this novel with the migrant experience in mind, it is clear that Wister was sensitive to a variety of different attitudes that Americans expressed toward the land. In this novel, the author makes use of at least five different environmental zones that are related to particular stages of development of civilization, a perception shared by many other nineteenth-century Americans. At one extreme, Wister describes the mountainous regions in the West, a territory inhabited by Indians who are not yet fully civilized, and a region in which the most violent and terrifying behavior could occur. Such violence was not necessarily appropriate, but it was not entirely unexpected. The second zone of environment exists where European civilization is first penetrating a new territory. Wister's discussion of ranch life in the West clearly indicates a territory in which civilization has not yet fully emerged, and yet there is more control over behavior than in the mountain regions. Ranch life is quite clearly distinguished from life on the farm, an even more settled and orderly kind of existence. Families, with women and children, can be found in farming communities, which also contain such institutions as churches or schools. Even small urban areas can be found in the midst of farm territory.

Wister distinguishes, however, between new farm regions in the West and older, more settled agricultural communities in the East when he describes a journey back to Vermont in which the hero is to be introduced to the family of his bride-to-be. There is clearly a stuffiness, if not a rigidity, in the territories settled for several generations compared to the freer social forms and expectations in the newly settled land in the West. Although he does not write extensively about urban areas, Wister does introduce the presence of the city in American society in a rather interesting fashion. At one point in the book, the ranchhands are required to take a herd of cattle out of the unsettled regions in the West and deliver them to the stockyards in the city. The city is portrayed in this brief passage as a place that can lure people away from a more appropriate environment. The Virginian, who has been placed in charge of this expedition, is expected to get his fellow ranchhands out of the city and back to the purer, more wholesome rural environment before they are led astray by the corrupting lures of the urban environment.

Perhaps the most famous novel that deals with migration as a fundamental part of the American experience is John Steinbeck's *Grapes of Wrath,* a story that attempts to capture the trauma of the Oklahoma residents forced out of that state by the dust bowl conditions of the 1930s, and lured westward with the hopes of a better future in the agricultural regions of California. Walter Stein's history of the dust-bowl migration is one of several studies that show that Steinbeck distorted the actual historical picture somewhat. On the one hand, Oklahoma was only one of several states that sent migrants westward, not only to California but also to Oregon and Washington. Perhaps more important, Californians were not as universally hostile to the arrival of the migrants from Oklahoma as Steinbeck suggests. Not all the Okies suffered the way the Jode family did. In addition, it is evident that the ultimate success in California of many of these families lay not in their ability to acquire land in the fertile Imperial valley or get work picking crops at decent wages, but rather depended on their willingness and ability to adjust to urban life and find work in factories, particularly as southern California industry expanded in the early years of World War II.

The *Grapes of Wrath* is one of the few novels that historians actually have consciously referred to in exploring the reality of the migrant experience. But it should be evident to anyone who reads western fiction or the fiction associated with immigration that a fuller attention to this body of literature, and a conscious effort to develop links between that literature and the historical record, would be most rewarding.

Nineteenth- and twentieth-century novels that are either set in cities or are about city life also deserve mention. Such works often catch as effectively as historical scholarship the antithetical ideas of Americans about their urban environments. Clearly, many Americans found cities attractive, because they moved to cities and stayed there. Cities were places of economic opportunity, and of excitement and adventure as well. There can be no doubt also that rural areas were frequently dirty, lonely, and full of hard work for many Americans. At the same time, cities were perceived as dangerous and threatening to the physical health and well-being of potential migrants, to the moral character of the people who lived there, and so, ultimately, to the future of

American civilization, which was believed to depend on a certain amount of virtue within the American people.

Theodore Dreiser's novel, *Sister Carrie,* chronicles the moral decline of a young, adventurous woman from rural Wisconsin, first in Chicago, and then eventually in New York City. This decline occurs in the context of hard and unappealing labor, and a rather callous disregard for Carrie's happiness and security by members of her family who were already in Chicago. The story is one that touched on Americans' concerns with how a young woman without sufficient social controls to reinforce appropriate moral behavior was vulnerable to her own instincts for pleasure, and the vices that the city presented to her. It also raised questions about the moral qualities of urban economics and family life. Richard Wright's powerful novel, *Native Son,* is also set in Chicago, and here, too, a young American named Bigger Thomas is reduced to extreme unhappiness in the large, throbbing, bewildering urban environment. In this instance the person who falls by the wayside is a young, black male who is unable to adjust to the different lifestyle of upper-middle class, white Americans.

Although they have considerably less literary merit than the works of Dreiser and Wright, Horatio Alger's novels, such as *Ragged Dick* or *Mark, the Match Boy,* are also set in America's cities and the contrast they offer reflects the ambiguous attitudes that Americans had toward urban life. His protagonists geneally come out much better than either Sister Carrie or Bigger Thomas. Alger shared the view that a city was a place of potential danger for the young in nineteenth- and early twentieth-century America; his stories are full of boys and young men who have been corrupted in one way or another by the hectic pace and lack of effective social control in urban America. However, his stories have at least one individual who does succeed in overcoming or avoiding the worst of the lures and dangers of the urban environment. Frequently, the success of an Alger hero, such as Ragged Dick, depends as much on accidents of fate as on strength of character.

Although the novel, *1984,* by British author George Orwell, is set in England, it is a story that has received considerable attention in the United States for obvious reasons. *1984* is the ultimate urban world, in which corruption has been extended to its fullest imaginable extent. Individual worth and dignity have been effectively destroyed, and freedom and opportunity have been eliminated. One of the ironies about the attraction of *1984* is that many nineteenth-century attitudes are reversed in this novel. One of the appeals of urban life to nineteenth-century Americans was that they were able to escape from the constant observation in a small town or village to find privacy, anonymity, and personal freedom in the city. In contrast, in *1984,* it is the urban area where conformity and continual observation are present. Individuality and freedom for personal expression can only be found in rural areas or on the fringes of the urban environment.

A final novel worth noting is Mark Twain's *Connecticut Yankee in King Arthur's Court,* a complex and fascinating story that reflects on the ultimate impossibility of imposing urban technology and the values associated with a technological society on a traditional, rural population. Twain may be unusual in having a greater sympathy for urban values and attitudes than some of his contemporary authors, but he is still fully aware of the conflict present in his society between new, urban lifestyles and the values and attitudes of rural America.

Anyone familiar with American literature surely will recognize that my references here only touch on the tip of a huge iceberg of novels and poetry, to say nothing of drama, that reflects the tremendously important, creative stimulus that migration and the ensuing human problems involved in adapting to new environments, attitudes, and values have brought to American literature. It should also be apparent that literature offers valuable opportunities for increasing our understanding of the meaning of migration in transforming Americans' lives.

5. MIGRATION AND AMERICA'S HISTORY

It would be difficult, if not impossible, to sum up completely what is known about past patterns of migration. Certainly, the topic is one of the central themes in American history and requires a variety of skills and perspectives in order to bring out the full meaning of the subject in all its manifestations. By way of conclusion, then, we will now return briefly to one overriding issue in American history. Is there an American history, or only histories of Americans? Much of the material examined so far shows that Americans came from many different lands bringing with them a wide variety of cultural heritages and values, and have not yet blended into one broad culture. Indeed, sectional and regional differences, and even more local divisions, continue to play an important role in American society, as they have since the seventeenth century. Because the emphasis has been so overwhelmingly on diversity, it is worth making a few comments on some factors that may reduce, if not eliminate, those factors that have divided us. This has been discussed more extensively in my book, *Revolutions in Americans' Lives.*

In the nineteenth century, many travelers observed what they thought was an American character. Both visitors from abroad and Americans touring their own country described Americans as being inquisitive, talkative, concerned with money and education, and prone to violence. These characteristics may simply reflect Americans responses to the problems of living with neighbors who had different values, and so could only be impressed by and evaluated through conversation and conspicuous consumption. Education, which contributed to efforts to control an uncertain world, did not always buffer friction arising from conflicting values sufficiently to avoid violence. In homogeneous societies, rituals and modes of expression that do not depend on words can provide the mechanism to establish one's own worth and that of strangers, and the means for resolving conflicts. The multiplicity of cultures that divided Americans made communication difficult on any but the most overt level, and may actually have fostered misunderstanding between people who interpreted symbolic actions in opposite ways. Thus, the American character may have been the product of a pluralistic society with special needs in order to maintain a minimum degree of internal stability.

Nonetheless, it appears that in the nineteenth century certain values and patterns of behavior were common among Americans, even though these values and actions were either residual or were made necessary by the extraordinary diversity of American society. Sharing common values and patterns of behavior is one definition of a common culture, and so the possibility exists that, however different from older European civilizations, America had at least some elements of a common history. The need to study the values and behavior that united and divided Americans suggests that anthropology may make the next significant contribution to our understanding of migration and of migrants in America's past, present, and future.

In the twentieth century, transportation networks and national media, ranging from magazines to radio and television networks, have created both a national economy with common material goods, and many more shared experiences than were possible in the past. The whole country can participate, even if only as observers, in political conventions, major sports events, and natural and human disasters. Furthermore, patterns of migration also have contributed to the blending of American society in the twentieth century. Immigration from abroad is significantly less than it was at the start of the twentieth century, in terms of both absolute numbers and migrants as a proportion of the total population. Furthermore, patterns of internal migration have provided greater mixing of the population in the twentieth century than before, breaking down some long-standing regional distinctions. However, not all regional differences have completely disappeared, because even the relatively new migration out of the North into the Sun Belt areas follows three distinct routes as Florida, Texas, and California all draw their populations from different parts of the North.

There is little doubt that the divisions that permeated American society in the latter half of the nineteenth century are subsiding. But will they disappear altogether, or will Americans ultimately divide themselves into three or four major segments by religion, region, or race? If a significant majority were to emerge and persist, might that majority impose a tyranny over a smaller, but perhaps much more obvious minority? This has rarely been a serious possibility in a widely fragmented society. From its origins, American history has been dominated by patterns of migration, and it is clear that the story of movement and its consequences for American society is not yet complete.

Chapter 5

Demographic Change and Family Life in American History: Some Reflections

Demography and Families

Demographic history has many connections with other aspects of American history. Politics, society, and the economy have all been affected by the extraordinary demographic changes that have been discussed to this point. However, no aspect of American life has been more profoundly influenced by the demographic structures and changes which have been discussed than the family. By the middle of the nineteenth century, Americans were already debating what was happening and what ought to happen to their families. That debate continues today, often with passion and nostalgia for family patterns that exist more in myth than in history. Therefore, a final chapter on the interactions between demographic events and trends and the nature of American families seems an appropriate way to conclude this volume.

One of the most obvious links between demography and the family is that the central life events of birth, death, marriage, and migration occur within the context of family life. Marriage, for example, frequently marks the passage of a young man or woman out of one family into another. The newly formed family becomes a new reproductive unit for society, since throughout American history most children have been born within families. Death is not always as directly linked to family life as marriage or childbirth, but this most fundamental of all changes frequently occurs within the context of the family. Likewise, migration may be common among isolated individuals, but frequently migrants have been part of a family moving either together or sequentially, with one family member leading the way to a new community, to be followed at a future time by the others.

The central life events experienced by most people in a society not only occur within families but also are controlled by families and alter family living as well. In the past, already existing families often controlled the creation of new families by marriage, partly to help mark the transition of the young to adulthood, and partly to limit the number of potential reproductive units laying claim to scarce resources. Similarly, the sexual activity of children often was expected to be regulated, if not completely postponed, by parents until children had reached a certain age. Death was not managed by families as effectively as some other aspects of demographic behavior, although in the twentieth century parents generally are expected to provide immunities available to children through medical attention. Nevertheless, death can alter families by removing members from the household, sometimes in a fashion that can be quite abrupt and unexpected. In addition, family members often provide support and comfort both for the dying and for each other to make the resulting transition as easy as possible. Finally, migration obviously alters families by both increasing and decreasing the numbers of people who live together, and by changing the environment in which family life takes place. In turn, the needs of families to send sons or daughters out into the world to seek their fortunes, or perhaps even to send a father off in search of a new community where the family might better prosper helps to shape the size and direction of streams of migration.

The expectations that the young acquire about having children, facing death, marrying, and moving, and the interpretations that they assign to their actual experiences with these phenomena frequently are connected to values that are taught by and implemented through families. Given the undeniably pleasant effects of sexual relationships, families have been remarkably effective in limiting, if not completely curtailing, sexual activity outside of marriage. One of the most remarkable aspects of life in seventeenth- and early eighteenth-century New England was the extent to which young men and women allowed their families to dictate the age at which they might marry by means of control over property, even where a community existed in the midst of large amounts of land on which new families could have set up housekeeping. In the past, parents have paid attention to preparing children to accept not only their own mortality, but also the fact that eventually their parents would depart from the face of the earth. The capacity to handle this major transition in an acceptable psychological fashion is perhaps one of the most important lessons that every child should learn. The values taught by one generation to another have sometimes reflected either myth or the past more than current demographic realities. Maris Vinovskis, for example, has suggested that nineteenth-century Americans often assumed that they faced a much harsher future than was warranted, according to his analysis of the mortality statistics of the time. Thus, families help to celebrate, mourn, and give recognition to major transitions in the life of every person brought about by their own demographic experiences and those of individuals closely associated to them.

A second major link between demographic history and the history of the family comes through the sources that demographers rely on for the study of past patterns of population. Family reconstitution, a technique that has been fundamental in allowing historians and demographers to describe and examine demographic behavior in the past, is a very close cousin of genealogy. Both of these techniques depend on the ability of a student to piece together from lists of births, marriages, and deaths an array of details about individual families. The genealogist may be interested in tracing his or her lineage back into the past, whereas the demographer or historian may have no special interest in a particular family name. Nonetheless, family reconstitution requires skills that are remarkably close to those of individuals interested in the study of particular families. In addition, demographic history becomes especially interesting when the demographic patterns of particular families can be linked to other aspects of family life through tax lists, church rolls, voting lists, and other documents recording the relationships of individuals in a particular community. A number of seventeenth- and eighteenth-century New England communities have been studied in this fashion, including Andover, Massachusetts, in the colonial period, and Concord, Massachusetts, during the Revolution. Mary Ryan's similar work on Utica, New York, in the nineteenth century will be examined shortly.

Censuses, in which information is recorded by household or family head, also provide important links between demographic and family history. The same records that provide data about population totals and age and sex composition on a large scale also may enable the researcher to explore such fascinating topics as the geographic and social mobility of individual families, the extent of fertility control within a population, and the size and structure of families at any particular point in time.

Finally, it should be noted that many of the important issues in family history require at least a basic knowledge of demographic patterns if they are to be understood. Scholars interested in the extent and nature of patriarchal control over families in the past must take into account such basic demographic phenomena as the number of children for which a father might have to provide, as well as how marriage patterns might reflect the control of one generation over another. Women's roles within families and society at large have been profoundly influenced by the number of children a woman might expect to have, at what ages she might expect to have them, and how early she might cease to bear children. Similarly, the migration of young women from rural New England into the textile towns in eastern Massachusetts during the mid-nineteenth century is of interest not only because of its effect on the demographic structure of those towns but also because of what it tells about the willingness of families to let their daughters leave home earlier than in previous generations, and may, in fact, have influenced the attitudes those women brought to the relationships they formed later on in their lives.

Family historians often have been interested in the changing economic roles of families in society in the nineteenth and early twentieth centuries. Although many of the new roles were clearly related to economic structures and modes of production that were unfamiliar in the eighteenth century, basic demographic changes were also important in creating new relationships. Rural families moved into urban environments to take up new and often unfamiliar jobs. As the number of children in the family declined, women may have found themselves freer to pursue work outside the home. Improved life expectancy at the end of the nineteenth century was accompanied by better health. This made it possible for the individual members of the nation's work force to be on the job more regularly and to be better able to provide a full day's work simply because they felt better. This, in turn, meant that many families were no longer as exposed to the threat of uncertain wages simply because they could count on family members being able to work. Families were increasingly protected from the catastrophic results of epidemic illness and death. Business cycles became more important in determining a family's fortune; more and more American families prospered and suffered together.

Given the close links between demographic history and the history of the family, it would be possible to write a complete book exploring the many and varied connections. Since that is neither possible nor desirable in the context of this volume, only two broad points will be explored. First, it is interesting to examine how thinking about the nature of families has evolved over the last two decades, providing more sophisticated and useful means of analyzing both family and demographic processes. After this has been done, some of the effects that the major demographic transitions of the last two centuries have brought to family life will be examined.

Thinking about Families

Since 1960, historians, demographers, and sociologists have altered the ways in which they think about families. Two decades ago, most families in the past were commonly though to have been extended. That is, three or more generations, and perhaps brothers, sisters, and cousins as well, all were assumed to live closely together. The explanation for the much smaller families, consisting typically of a husband and wife and their own children, that were found in the mid-twentieth century in the United States, was that such nuclear families had emerged in response to industrial society. We now know that this is not ture. Nuclear families have been common for the last three or four centuries.

In thinking about the family, it is clear that the word "family" has several possible meanings, each of which may be appropriate to particular forms of family or demographic history, but all need to be more precisely defined. There are at least four commonly used definitions. One is that of a reproductive unit consisting of a husband and wife and their children. A second definition of a family is frequently used in conjunction with census data and involves the concept of a household—that is, a group of people who reside together in the same dwelling. A somewhat broader definition of a household that is appropriate for certain times and places in American history involves all those individuals who lived in close proximity to each other, engaging in some common economic pursuit under the direction of one particular individual. The most clearcut example of this kind of family is the plantation in the South when slavery was still common. Although slaves and their white masters rarely, if ever, actually resided in the same house, the whites frequently referred to the whole group as a family. Whether black slaves considered the residents of the plantation to be all one family is another matter. A third definition of the family involves the notion of kinship, that is, all those individuals to whom we consider ourselves somehow or other related. In English, we refer to them as fathers and mothers, children, brothers and sisters, grandparents, uncles and aunts, or cousins of some sort. Records in other languages from other cultures sometimes use words that may be translated directly into English with little distortion of meaning, but it is important to be sensitive to possible subtle, but significant, differences among cultures in the variety of words they use to describe kinship when studying the family patterns among Indians, Afro-Americans, and non-English speaking Europeans. For example, an older, and presumably wiser, male of an earlier generation might be referred to by a word that could appropriately be translated into English as "father," "uncle," or "wise elder." However, each of those meanings in English is quite different. In addition, there is a more limited group of kin to which the term family is also applied, namely those individuals to whom we would turn for assistance in time of trouble. In general, the circle of kin with whom we have expectations of mutual obligations and responsibilities is somewhat smaller than the array of individuals we recognize ourselves to be related to through blood or marriage. How wide this circle is depends on time, culture, and the intimate history of individual families.

The simplest way of looking at families is by descriptions or pictures of structures or patterns at a particular moment in time. Thus, demographers and family historians have studied the number of children ever born to a particular husband and wife by the end of their marriage. Likewise, censuses provide snapshots of what households looked like in terms of size and structures in a given year. Each of these views of the family has its own merits, yet both are limited because they provide no sense of how families have grown, changed, and declined over a long period of time. The children born to an eighteenth-century American couple may have arrived in that family over the span of twenty to twenty-five years, a much longer period of time than is spent in childbearing in the second half of the twentiety century. Death, marriage, and migration might have worked at a much slower pace to shrink the same family. Thus, it has become clear that static views of the family are not always adequate either for demographic or family historians. Family life was and is a process of change and adaptation to both the arrival and departure of new individuals, and the growth and development of the individuals who remain within the family for a prolonged period of time.

The value of taking a dynamic rather than a static view of family life has been brought home through several important studies. One of the most interesting, by Lutz Berkner, examined eighteenth-century European families. By grouping households according to the age of the head of the household, Berkner discovered that, although the size of families remained remarkably constant, their structures changed rather dramatically with the age of the head. Therefore, he argued, families passed through distinct stages depending on how long the family had been in existence and its ability to command economic resources within a community. Berkner raised the question of which, if any, of the various stages of the family was closest to the ideal. Although he agreed that nuclear families were quite common in eighteenth-century

Europe, he pointed out that they may not, in fact, have been the preferred way to live. Possibly, families in which there were three generations or perhaps a boarder present were, for one reason or another, more preferred by the people of that time than the nuclear pattern, but demographic conditions made it difficult for most families to exist in the ideal state. Berkner also concluded that most individuals who lived more than a few years would have experienced a variety of family types over the course of their lives and so could not be analyzed as having been born, brought up, and matured within a particular household structure.

The explorations of household structures by this author, using censuses compiled in late-seventeenth-century New York and in Louisiana in the 1760s have reenforced the conclusion that it is necessary to pay attention to the development of households over time rather than to look at them as static units. For example, small households often reflected a variety of circumstances. A family recorded in a census as containing three people may be composed of a young husband and wife who have just had their first child, or, such a family could be a husband and wife who have had a number of children, all but one of whom had died from endemic or epidemic diseases. Finally, a three-person household may simply be an older couple with only one of their children still living with them. In Louisiana, in the 1760s, several communities studied by Andrew Walsh and myself had families that were surprisingly small. Close study showed that these communities were relatively new, and hence were composed of families in which most householders were relatively young. Older communities with older households had larger families. Although the average size of the household in the new communities remained remarkably constant over the span of three or four years, relatively few of the individual households remained unchanged. In one instance, it was possible to trace fifty-two families between 1766 and 1769. Of these fifty-two households, only four remained unaltered in both size and membership. The other forty-eight changed in size and/or composition in the space of three years.

Students of seventeenth-century Chesapeake families, such as Lois Carr and Lorena Walsh, or Darrett and Anita Rutman, have reenforced the importance of examining the development of households as well as their structures at any point in time. In early Virginia and Maryland, households frequently were complex combinations of parts of previous families coexisting with new members of the current household. A simple structural analysis of a seventeenth-century

Chesapeake household might provide evidence of a husband and wife and four children living in a household. But with a dynamic perspective, we might learn that this was the second or third marriage for both husband and wife. In addition, the four children, instead of all being born to that particular marriage, might include a child of the father's, a child of the mother's, each from a previous marriage, one child who was the product of this union, and a fourth child who might be an indentured servant or the child of one of the brothers or sisters of the husband or wife who had been taken in either to learn an occupation or because of dislocation in that child's own immediate family.

The need to introduce a dynamic perspective to the study of the family has led historians to choose among several forms of life-cycle analysis. Figure 10 summarizes some of the most fruitful approaches. After using this diagram to consider how thinking about family history has become more complex and sophisticated over the last several decades, there are some brief comments on how readers might use the model presented here as a starting point for their own personal study of family history.

One dynamic perspective is to study the life cycle of the individual. Complete or partial life cycles of individuals of four successive generations have been represented in the figure by the lines labeled "Grandparent," "Parent," "First Child," "Child of First Child," and "Last Child." They are intended to be studied in conjunction with the rectangle in the middle of the figure, labeled "Family Cycle," but can, for the moment, be considered by themselves. Historians looking at family life from this perspective have examined how individuals move through a series of stages and changes from being a very small child, to an adolescent, to a young adult, to a mature adult, and ultimately to an older adult. This can be done with greater or less sophistication, examining, among other things, various changes an individual experiences in family and social roles as he or she moves from one age level to another. With data from several decades or centuries, it is possible to study how various stages of development have expanded and contacted or perhaps even multiplied over time. One important result of these kinds of studies has been an increasing awareness that, at least in the past, the life cycle of the individual depended greatly on the sex, race, and cultural heritage of the individual. In the twentieth century, individual life cycles have become increasingly similar.

A second life cycle approach studies not individuals but families. This technique is based on the concept that families go through stages

Figure 10. Dynamic approaches to studying families.

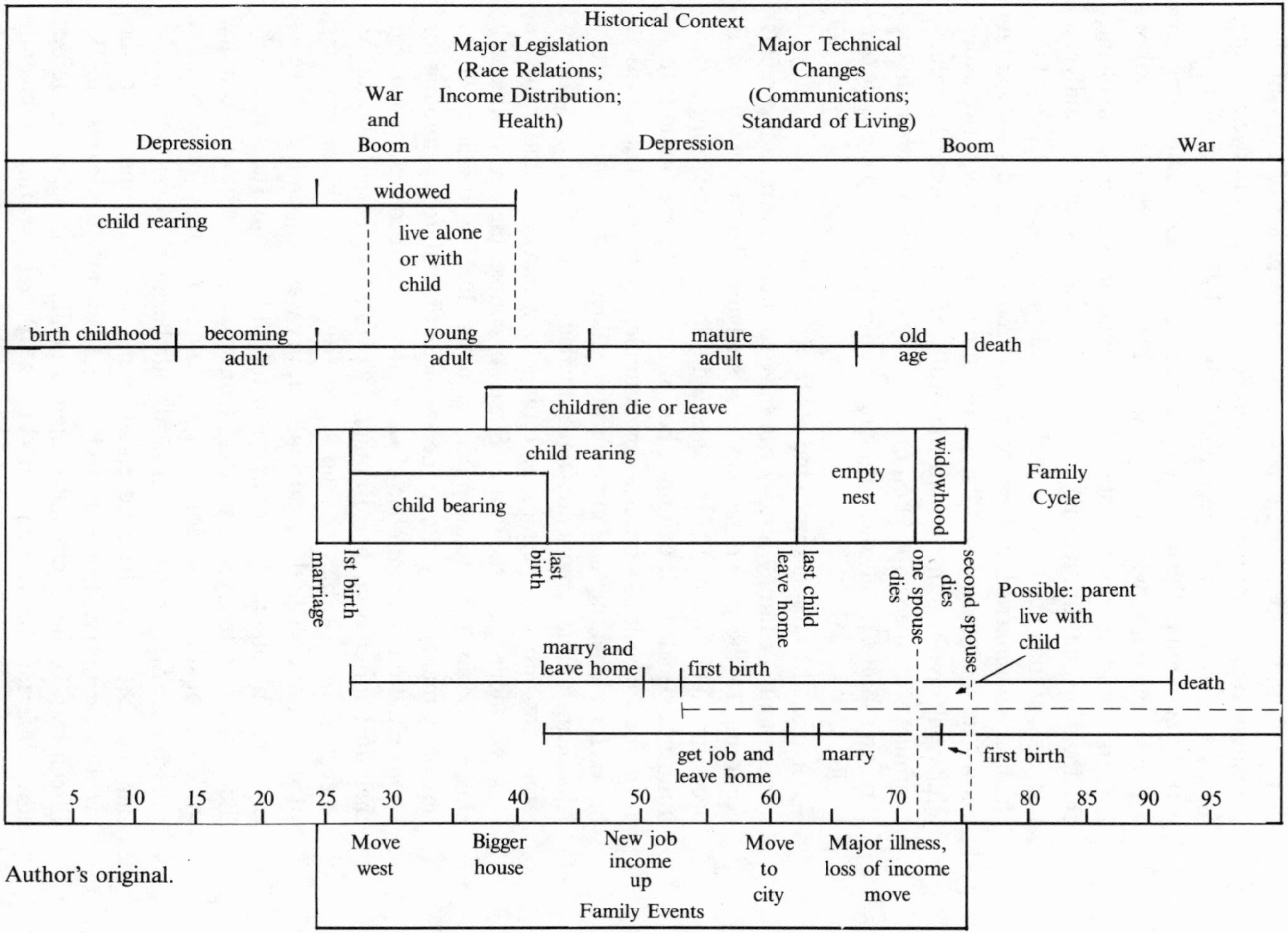

Source: Author's original.

that profoundly affect the experiences and behavior of each of the individual family members. One simple form of the life cycle of the family, represented by the rectangle in the middle of Figure 10, begins with the creation of the family via marriage, followed by a brief stage in which husband and wife live together without children. The arrival of the first child marks the start of a much longer stage involving childbearing and childrearing, two closely related aspects of family life that may or may not be separated for analytic purposes. When all the children have married, moved, or died, parents are faced with what is known as the "empty nest" stage of family life in which two older adults will live together. With the death of one spouse, the family continues with the widowhood of either the husband or wife until the surviving spouse finally dies, bringing to an end the complete cycle of a family.

Anyone who adopts some kind of life-cycle analysis in their study of demographic or family history will have to make several adjustments according to the period he or she is studying. To begin with, it is necessary to be aware of both stages and transitions. Regarding stages, it must be decided, for example, how many significant divisions there are in the life cycle of a family. For example, is it useful to differentiate between childbearing and childrearing? Students of twentieth-century American families frequently have divided the childrearing stage of family life into two periods according to whether or not there are children under six in the family. Six is, of course, the age at which all children begin to attend public school. Such a division would obviously make little sense in the absence of mandatory schooling for young children. The number of stages that need to be examined and their duration may change dramatically over a long period of time. As is evident from Tables IX and X, the duration of the childrearing stage of family life in the eighteenth century was frequently forty years or more. In contemporary America, the childrearing stage of family life is at least ten years shorter. Conversely, in eighteenth-century America, death was so common a phenomenon that many couples missed the empty nest stage of family life because at least one spouse had died before all the children left home. In the second half of the twentieth century, husbands and wives frequently can expect ten to fifteen years of life together after their last child has departed. Consider how different the rectangle in Figure 10, representing eighteenth century expectations, would look from one depicting a twentieth century family.

Transition points are as important to study as the stages those transitions define. In recent years, John Modell and others have discovered major changes over the centuries in the age at which individuals experienced transitions, the number of transitions they may go through, the sequence of those transitions, the amount of time between one transition and another, and how common all transitions are to a particular generation. Consider, for example, what it means for a young person to leave home. In modern America, individuals frequently leave home to attend school. After they have graduated from college, they may then get their first job and marry several years later. This sequence is common for both sons and daughters. A century ago, however, a daughter might occasionally leave home for several years to take a job. Going to college for a girl was highly unusual. More likely, she left her parents only upon marriage. A son, on the other hand, might leave home to take a job, marrying relatively quickly thereafter. In fact, historians have discovered a remarkable tendency in the twentieth century for all young people to experience all the transitions that mark the passage between being a child in one's

Table IX. Median Age of Wives at Stages of the Life Cycle of the Family

Stage of the Life Cycle of the Family	Wives Born		
	Before 1786 (Quakers)	1880–1889	1920–1929
A. First marriage	20.5*	21.6	20.8
B. Birth of last child	37.9	32.9	30.5
C. Marriage of last child	60.2	56.2	52.0
D. Death of first spouse to die	50.9	57.0	64.4

*The overall patterns of marriage, birth of last child, and duration of marriage seem to have been much the same, from one group to another. To the extent that one group was different from the other two, it is the wives born between 1920 and 1929 who seem to be somewhat unusual and not the Quakers.

SOURCE: Robert V. Wells, "Demographic Change and the Life Cycle of American Families," Appendix. Reprinted from *The Journal of Interdisciplinary History,* II (1971): 281–282, with permission of *The Journal of Interdisciplinary History* and The M.I.T. Press, Cambridge, Massachusetts. Copyright 1971, by the Massachusetts Institute of Technology and the editors of *The Journal of Interdisciplinary History.*

Table X. Median Length of Selected Stages of the Life Cycle of the Family (in years)

Stage of the Life Cycle of the Family	Wives Born		
	Before 1786 (Quakers)	1880–1889	1920–1929
1. Childbearing	17.4	11.3	9.7
2. Childrearing	39.7	34.6	31.2
3. Duration of marriage	30.4	35.4	43.6
4. Old age together	– 9.3	0.8	12.4
5. Widowhood			
Female	13.7	18.7	—
Male	12.5	14.2	—
6. Marriage of last child to death of last spouse, when last is			
Female	4.4	19.5	—
Male	3.2	15.0	—

The above table was derived as follows:
Table X.

Line 1 = Line B – Line A

Line 2 = Line C – Line A

Line 3 = Line D – Line A

Line 4 = Line D – Line C

(Lines 1–4: From Table IX)

Line 5 = The figures for the husbands and wives born before 1786 were calculated directly from my data. For the others, see Glick and Parke, "New Approaches," 195.

Line 6 = Line 4 and Line 5

SOURCE: Robert V. Wells, "Demographic Change and the Life Cycle of American Families," Appendix. Reprinted from *The Journal of Interdisciplinary History,* II (1971): 281–282, with permission of *The Journal of Interdisciplinary History* and The M.I.T. Press, Cambridge, Massachusetts. Copyright 1971, by the Massachusetts Institute of Technology and the editors of *The Journal of Interdisciplinary History.*

parents' household to establishing a household of one's own. The young who go through the entire sequence do so more quickly than was common in the late nineteenth century.

Because most life-cycle approaches seek to define the average experience, it is important to ask how common was the average pattern. Historians can most easily describe what the average life cycle of a family or of an individual might look like. However, in periods in which there were wide variations in age at marriage, the number of children born to a family, and the expectation of life of any one individual, the expected pattern might differ quite significantly from an individual's actually experience. Peter Uhlenberg, for example, has discovered that in the nineteenth century, only about one of every five females born actually passed through the entire life cycle of an average family. Although a few women lived long lives without marrying, and fewer still were divorced, death commonly intruded to make it impossible for the others to experience the full array of transitions and stages. In a family with six children, the life cycle of the first born child was quite different from that of the sixth child, both in terms of the number of people that child had to relate to in the life of the family and the conditions under which he or she might be raised. Not surprisingly, first borns generally had a greater expectation of having parents around through most of their lives than would a sixth child who was born when the parents had already reached their early forties. The lines labeled "First Child" and "Last Child" in Figure 10 can be looked at in conjunction with the "Family Cycle" in the middle in order to make this difference clear.

In order to take into account these complexities, historians of the family have begun to study what is termed the life course rather than the life cycle. This approach recognizes that individual lives do not intersect in equal ways with family life cycles. Even though two individuals may have been alive during the mid-nineteenth century, and were members of the same family, their lives may have been quite different simply because one of them was a first born and one of them was born last in a large family.

Recognition that different historical circumstances can further influence the way the life cycle of individuals and the life cycle of families intersect to produce different life courses adds an equally important perspective to this mode of analysis. Thus, every generation presumably has its own unique experiences. For example, husbands and wives who married in the early 1930s faced quite different economic prospects than those couples who married in the midst of

World War II. In turn, couples who married in the early 1950s had prospects for a stable, prosperous family life that were much more promising than those facing the cohorts of the early 1930s or 1940s. This author's study of Quaker families in the late eighteenth century has indicated that their childbearing patterns changed rather abruptly about the onset of the American Revolution, suggesting that the generation immediately preceding the Revolution saw no reason to curtail childbearing, but those who married and began to create their own family in the midst of the revolutionary situation found reason to try and control the size of the family. The top of Figure 10, labeled "Historical Context," presents some of the possible national events that might affect the life cycles of individuals and families. At the bottom, the rectangle titled "Family Events," includes some of the possible elements of a family's private history that might also affect members of a family in different ways.

Although there have been relatively few studies exploring the interactions of individual life cycles with family life cycles taking into account the specific historical context, it is obvious that the analysis produced by such a perspective is much more sophisticated and much more complex than that involving a simple description of the static structures of the size of a family or household at any one point in time. That is not to say that simple static descriptions do not have their merit, for under certain circumstances they describe the way in which a society is put together. Nonetheless, over the last several decades scholars have become increasingly sophisticated in their understanding of both the factors that shape an individual's development within his or her family, and how family life can change because of historical circumstances and because of the conditions an individual experiences within the family in the course of his or her lifetime.

Figure 10 depicts the dynamic perspective on individuals and families in a very general form. Its immediate purpose was to make some of the preceding discussion clearer. However, readers should be able to use this model to gain a fuller understanding of the lives of some real people. For example, try creating the equivalent diagram for your own family. If genealogies are available, the life cycles of different historical families can be drawn. On a more abstract level, readers could diagram families and individuals in which the transitions and stages vary in number and duration, and place them in real historical contexts. Other possibilities should suggest themselves, including differences arising from sex or cultural heritage.

Not all aspects of family history that are closely related to demographic history make use of the life-cycle perspective. Two of the most interesting recent works in family history have a basic demographic core, but have somewhat different theoretical orientations. One is Carl Degler's recent book, *At Odds,* in which the author argues a basic conflict has existed over the last two centuries between women's needs and efforts to develop themselves as individuals and the demands that women subordinate themselves to the interest of their family. As part of his examination of the tensions that emerged between women and their families, Degler found it desirable to explore in some detail the extent to which fertility was controlled between the late eighteenth century and the present, and the means by which that control was achieved. It is of some significance that women had a great deal of influence over the introduction of contraception, and were not entirely dependent on men and male-controlled modes of birth control.

In her impressive study of the origins of middle-class family structures and values in Oneida County in New York between 1790 and 1865, Mary Ryan has paid as much attention to basic demographic behavior as Degler. Although Ryan's main concern is the articulation and dissemination of a new set of values that helped to define middle-class society, and to perpetuate that society into the late nineteenth and early twentieth centuries, she has remained sensitive to the basic demographic changes that accompanied the changes in attitudes and perceptions. Thus, she provides detailed explorations not only of migration patterns into emerging industrial communities but also of such basic demographic structures as age and sex composition, and household patterns. The evolution of Oneida society is a superb example of how demographic structures interacted with family patterns and cultural values to alter the way in which Americans went about their lives. Ryan argues effectively that the emergence of new values by 1865, although shaped by the demographic changes that occurred over the previous three-quarters of a century, were by no means the only values that could have worked within the contours of the basic demographic structures. Thus, she demonstrates clearly that the connection between value and demographic behavior is close but is not deterministic. The men and women who lived in Oneida County in the early nineteenth century had to adapt to new demographic structures and did so successfully, but they did so on their terms rather than as pawns in some kind of gigantic demographic chess game.

Demographic Change and Family Life

What have been the effects of major demographic changes between the eighteenth century and the present on family life? It is not possible here to deal with all of the possible and probable results, and with the impact of demographic changes on the broader contours of American life in terms of the economy, politics, and society. However, some comment on a few of the major alterations in family life is possible.

When looking at the meaning of the fertility decline for American men and women between the eighteenth and the twentieth centuries, several points stand out. One of the most notable has been the decrease in the average size of households. In the late eighteenth century, an average household contained about six people. Today, households average around three individuals. Much of the difference is the result of the extraordinary decline in childbearing that occurred during the nineteenth and early twentieth centuries, although it will be noted shortly that there are other factors to be considered. In addition, the fact that an average couple had fewer children over the course of their life cycle has had several effects in terms of family life. Perhaps the most notable is that couples can anticipate the empty nest stage of the family cycle to be a much longer and more important part of their lives. With fewer children, childbearing ends at an earlier age, and the last child marries and leaves home when the mother and father are younger than was the case in the past.

What has been the impact on individual lives of this extraordinary reduction in childbearing? Obviously, having fewer children has put considerable less burden on American women in the twentieth century than was the case 200 years ago. Having two children as opposed to six has implications not only for a woman's health but also for the amount of time she will have to devote to the care and raising of others, at considerable sacrifice to her own personal development. As a result, women in the twentieth century are much freer to pursue whatever line of personal development they desire, whether that be a career in the business world or simply providing better maternal care.

From the point of view of the child, the reduction in fertility has had several significant effects. Obviously, a child in a two-person family ought to receive greater attention from his or her parents than one who grows up in the midst of eight or ten competitors for adult attention. The benefits of this depend on the character of the parents, but in general children will develop more rapidly and will acquire greater verbal and numerical skills as a result of greater contact with educated parents than they will if much of their contact is with children of only slightly differing age. A second less obvious but no less important benefit to a child is that women who have fewer children generally have children who are healthier. Thus, children in the twentieth century probably have benefitted in a physical as well as a psychological sense from being born into smaller families.

In addition, a combination of larger houses, made possible by extraordinary economic growth during the nineteenth and twentieth centuries, plus fewer children has meant that each member of an American family today generally has greater chances for privacy than was the case in the past. A rough rule of thumb to describe the change is that in the eighteenth century there were approximately two people for every room in a typical American house. By the second half of the twentieth century, this ratio has changed so that there are approximately two rooms per person. It would have been a rare child in the eighteenth century who could have expected his or her own separate bedroom to which to retire for whatever purposes he or she felt necessary. This is a quite common phenomenon today.

Improved life expectancy also has had a considerable impact on family life, both directly and through the better health that accompanies most reductions in the death rate. One obvious point is that families are less frequently disrupted by death. Whereas in seventeenth-century America, families commonly experienced abrupt dislocations because of epidemic and endemic diseases, in the twentieth century, a couple who marry can expect a long life together. Possibly, the rapid increase in divorce that began about 1890 is at least partially linked to this improvement in life expectancy simply because a husband or wife caught in an unpleasant marital situation could no longer hope for salvation through the death of the other spouse. The most dramatic increases in life expectancy have occurred during exactly the same period in which divorce has become more common in American society. This relationship is particularly interesting because, in general, improved life expectancy made families more stable or at least predictable; departures from the family are, in the twentieth century, more likely to be by choice, whether by divorce or migration, rather than by the chance appearance of smallpox, cholera, dysentery, influenza or diphtheria.

One trend of special interest to twentieth-century Americans has been the emergence of a much older society which has increased the possibility of grandparents being a regular part of the family. The increasingly older American population is primarily the result of declining fertility, which is the principle cause of changes in the age structure of any population, but it is also true that grandparents now live longer than was the case two hundred years ago. One might assume that the emergence of a sizable proportion of the population over the age of sixty (the change has been from approximately four percent in the eighteenth century to about twelve percent today) would mean that more households would include three generations, or possibly even four for relatively short periods of time. In fact, this does not seem to have occurred as often as might be expected. One explanation for this is simply that as life expectancy has improved older Americans have maintained much better health than was the case two hundred years ago, and so they are able to maintain their independence much longer than would have been normal in 1800 or 1850. In the early nineteenth century, the association between advanced age and physical disability would have been almost automatic; that no longer is true. As a result, older Americans are able to maintain their independence in separate households well up into their seventies and eighties. In fact, the dramatic increase in single-person households from seven percent in 1940 to twenty-three percent in 1980 is at least partially explainable by widows and widowers maintaining their households after their children have left home and their spouse has died, and not by young Americans leaving home early.

One other alternative that has emerged because of improved life expectancy deserves attention, although there is little evidence to indicate that this will be a major trend in American society. In the past, when life expectancy was short, any society that survived had to develop patterns of behavior that would guarantee relatively high levels of reproduction. When half of one generation might die before reaching marriageable ages, most of the survivors had to marry and have children. Any society that allowed significant deviations from this pattern would disappear if the birth rate fell below the death rate for any prolonged period. Since the death rate in the United States today is slightly under 9 per 1,000 people, compared to between 25 and 30 per 1,000 two hundred years ago, Americans can now experiment in alternate patterns of family living that once threatened the survival of society. The last two decades have seen considerable increase in communal families, in young men and women living together without marrying or having children, and in homosexual alliances. It seems doubtful that any of these patterns will significantly challenge, let alone replace, the age-old norm of heterosexual marriages leading to reproduction. Nonetheless, improved life expectancy makes it possible for individuals to experiment with alternate living styles without severely threatening the actual existence of their society. The major obstacle they will have to overcome is presented by those individuals who are worried, not about the physical survival of society, but about the need to protect the values that have been required to produce satisfactory levels of reproduction in the past. At issue is the extent to which the fundamental values of any society are inseparable from attitudes about marriage and childbearing. Are heterosexual, reproductive unions essential to the continuity of an American way of life?

The patterns of migration that have been so important in American demographic history also have had important effects on family life. The process of moving, whether across the Atlantic Ocean, from east to west across the United States, or into an urban environment, has frequently produced either permanent or temporary dislocations of families and households. Lasting changes in families occur when young men or women leave home as the result of marriage, especially since young women often also leave the communities in which they were raised to travel to the towns where their new husbands reside. Before slavery was abolished, black families were vulnerable to separation when whim or economic necessity led a white master to sell some of his people. A more temporary dislocation of families can result from serial migration, in which the head of the household leaves his or her family behind to establish housekeeping in a new community, and then over the span of several months or years will bring along the remaining family members. Under certain circumstances, serial migration can last over a number of years when an individual nuclear family becomes established in a particular community and then aids related families to move to that community. Migrants from abroad have used this pattern, as have families in New England in the late nineteenth century who assisted each other as they moved from one textile town to another.

In new communities, family sizes and structures have undergone rather interesting changes as the result of migration patterns. In towns that have just been established, or which have experienced rapid growth, household structures frequently differ from the normal American pattern by being both smaller and larger. The smaller families are often the temporary product of serial migration or relatively young householders, whereas unusually large households may be the result of newly arrived individuals boarding with families already resident in the town. Gradually, these initial distortions in family life disappear and life in the mature community settles into a fairly standard pattern of family existence. Often life in a more stable community has meant improved economic standing for those families that remain. This should not be too surprising because one of the significant motivations in migration, whether from across the Atlantic or from one town to another in the United States, has been the hope for economic prosperity.

In general, in both the nineteenth and twentieth centuries, families seldom have traveled any long distances in any one move, but because they move several times in the course of the family cycle, rather long distances have been covered in the life of one family. Thus, a household formed in Ohio in the early part of the nineteenth century could end up in Oregon, but only after stops in Illinois, Missouri, and Iowa along the way. Similarly, black migrants from the Georgia Sea Islands frequently moved onto the mainland, and then into Georgia's urban areas, before they began the trek north to New York City and a life style quite different from that which characterized rural Georgia. As was common throughout much of American history, the individual black males who pioneered this trek from the Sea Islands to the northern cities frequently brought along other members of their family after they were established in the northern urban environment.

Migration has also served to emphasize differences among various groups of families. This has happened in several ways. The occupational structures of an individual town has been one of the most important forces in selecting who might migrate to a particular community. For example, Lowell, Massachusetts, in the early nineteenth century, was characterized by highly unusual demographic and residential patterns because the cotton mills there recruited young single women who lived in housing provided by the mills themselves. Cohoes, a milltown a few miles north of Albany, New York, had an unusually high proportion of families headed by women because women who had lost a husband were able to maintain their families there since they were able to find work in the textile mills for both themselves and their older children. In other communities, they might not have been able to survive independently or keep their families together. In contrast, Homestead, Pennsylvania, a town slightly north of Pittsburgh, dominated by a steel mill, was characterized at the start of the twentieth century by families that were nuclear. In the case of Homestead, work in the steel millls was largely restricted to adult males, and so women and children frequently were not employed outside the home. At the same time, most steel mill workers had families with them.

Because the various groups of immigrants who arrived in the United States, each with their own set of attitudes and customs about family life, did not distribute themselves evenly across the country, family patterns in any one particular American community have differed considerably from those in another community depending on which immigrant group settled there. In Homestead, Pennsylvania, for example, Polish-born workers and their families generally spent their money in different patterns, amused themselves differently, and even ate differently than did American or English workers in the steel mills. In Buffalo, New York, Italian and Polish families responded quite differently to the same community. Virginia Yans-McLaughlin has shown that cultural preferences had as much to do with women working as the economic opportunities available in Buffalo. The very nature of the force producing migration from Europe might well affect family life. Irish immigrants of the 1840s and Jewish migrants from Russia in the 1890s frequently moved in family units, with no intention of returning to their original society because of either unhappy religious or economic prospects in the old world. In contrast, Italian and Chinese immigrants tended to be younger, single males who either brought families over much later or moved to the United States temporarily, with every intention of returning to the old country after they had made a satisfactory amount of money. As a result, stable patterns of family life were established much more quickly among Irish and Jewish immigrants than among the Chinese or Italians.

Although such communities were not numerous, nineteenth-century towns that incorporated utopian ideals often developed distinctive arrangements for and attitudes about family life. Shaker communities in western Massachusetts and eastern New York organized society around a life that basically denied the family. Men and women who were attracted to Shaker settlements were required to be celibate, and any kind of sexual or family relationship was generally discouraged. Shakers commonly lived in sexually segregated dormitories. In contrast, Oneida, also a utopian community in upstate New York, fostered the creation of much larger families, in which sexual relations were not only permitted but were encouraged. Men and women were no longer expected to be monogamous. Free love was an important value in this society, though it required rigorous forms of sexual relations in which self-control was considered essential as the means to achieving limited levels of reproduction. The Mormons, who migrated from New York to Utah, with stops in Missouri and Illinois, in order to preserve their religious integrity and escape persecution by their neighbors, also created distinct family patterns. The best known was the practice of polygamy, which allowed a Mormon man to have more than one wife. Not surprisingly, Mormon families were relatively large, not only because there was more than one wife able to bear children but also because Mormons espoused high fertility values. Although relatively few Americans actually practiced such unusual family patterns, these nineteenth-century experiments with new family forms attracted considerable attention because many Americans were aware of the major demographic changes going on around them and were involved in a widespread debate about whether they should be encouraged, discouraged, or ignored.

Migration has influenced how and when different branches of a family interact through a variety of mechanisms. As part of a highly mobile American society, family members had to accept separation as they moved considerable distances from each other. This has affected ties and relationships based on kinship. In the seventeenth century, kin were expected to provide considerable aid to one another, and this was possible so long as families lived relatively short distances apart. It is interesting, therefore, to ask what has happened in terms of kinship when one brother may live in New York City, his sister lives in San Francisco, and a third sibling resides in Dallas? On the surface, it would appear that kinship ties should have been significantly reduced as the result of such distances among families. On the other hand, technological changes in our ability to communicate rapidly via the telephone and in our ability to travel long distances in relatively short periods of time may mean that kinship ties have not been reduced as much as we might suspect. It is possible to telephone a relative across the country faster than you can walk next door to visit a neighbor. Similarly, it seldom takes more than seven or eight hours to cross the country by air today, a time that compares to a journey of twenty to thirty miles in the seventeenth or eighteenth centuries. The day-to-day and hour-to-hour contacts that were common in close-knit communities in the past may no longer exist, however, kinship ties have probably not been as dramatically altered by migration as one might expect. Probably interactions with one's kin now occur more often in the context of special events such as holidays, births, marriages, or deaths rather than in ongoing contact as part of daily activity. No doubt, choice plays a greater role in family contact under such circumstances. In addition, lines between family and community, once blurred when individuals lived in small towns or villages among cousins, uncles, and aunts, have perhaps been more sharply defined, so that we can identify what is public and what is private in our lives. However, these changes have not necessarily eliminated kinship ties but have only altered them.

Perhaps of greater consequence to the day-to-day existence of life of an American family has been the movement to suburban communities with the associated separation of economic and domestic activity. In the suburbs, frequently the adult males, and increasingly adult females, leave home to go to work elsewhere in the larger urban area. As a result, the home has become a place of recreation, rest, and retreat, rather than economic activity. The home is where economic goods are consumed rather than produced. In addition, whereas families on small farms frequently worked within eyesight of each other, if not necessarily at the same tasks, now family members are separated from each other for significant parts of the day. Each individual family member, whether husband, wife, or child, once he or she begins attending school, develops numerous contacts with individuals with whom the other members of the family seldom, if ever, interact. Thus, families in twentieth-century America are increasingly composed of individuals who both share a life, but who also have lives that are almost entirely separate from each other. This latter condition would have been extremely unusual two hundred years ago.

Conclusion

The effects of demographic changes on American family life already have been numerous and significant. Because the changes are not yet complete, and because Americans have not yet decided what new family patterns they consider to be desirable, considerable experimentation with, and debate over, new and old family patterns will continue over the next several decades. Nonetheless, in examining the relationship between demography and family life one overriding conclusion emerges. There is no such thing as *the* American family; there are only families in America that vary considerably according to the historical period in which they existed, the place in which they are located, and the class and cultural background of the individuals composing those families. We would do well not to be too rigid in our expectations about and interpretations of family life. Families have been, and will continue to be, a vital and important part of American society, but that vitality has come more from their capacity to adapt to remarkable changes in demographic and economic patterns than from any power to maintain rigid adherence to traditional patterns in the face of extraordinary changes. Lower levels of childbearing and improved life expectancy may make experimentation with new forms of family life more possible than it was in the past, but that does not mean that any new patterns will prove ultimately to be more desirable than older family relationships. It should be interesting to both observe and experience family life in America over the next several decades.

References and Readings

Chapter 1

Braudel, Fernand. *The Structures of Everyday Life: The Limits of the Possible*. Translated by Sian Richards. New York: Harper & Row, 1981.

Chapple, Elliot. *Culture and Biological Man: Explorations in Behavioral Anthropology*. New York: Holt, Rinehart and Winston, 1970.

Glass, David V., and D. E. C. Eversley, eds. *Population in History*. Chicago: Aldine Press, 1965.

Hollingsworth, T. H. *Historical Demography*. Ithaca, N.Y.: Cornell University Press, 1969.

Potter, J. "The Growth of Population in America, 1700–1870." In *Population in History,* edited by D. V. Glass and D. E. C. Eversley, pp. 631–688. Chicago: Aldine Press, 1965.

Twain, Mark. *A Connecticut Yankee in King Arthur's Court*. New York: Charles L. Webster & Co., 1889.

Vinovskis, Maris, ed. *Studies in American Historical Demography*. New York: Academic Press, 1979.

Wells, Robert V. "Family History and Demographic Transition." *Journal of Social History* 9 (1975): 1–19.

Wells, Robert V. *Revolutions in Americans' Lives: A Demographic Perspective on the History of Americans, Their Families, and Their Society*. Westport, Conn.: Greenwood Press, 1982.

Wrigley, E. A. *Population and History*. New York: McGraw-Hill, 1969.

Chapter 2

Byers, Edward. "Fertility Transition in a New England Commercial Center: Nantucket, Massachusetts, 1680–1840." *Journal of Interdisciplinary History* 13 (1982): 17–40.

Coale, Ansley J., and Norfleet W. Rives, Jr., "A Statistical Reconstruction of the Black Population of the United States, 1880–1970." *Population Index* 39 (1973): 3–36.

Coale, Ansley J., and Melvin Zelnik. *New Estimates of Fertility and Population in the United States.* Princeton, N.J.: Princeton University Press, 1963.

Crum, Frederick S. "The Decadence of the Native American Stock: A Statistical Study of Genealogical Records." *American Statistical Association Journal* 14 (1916–1917): 215–222.

Cutright, Phillips, and Edward Shorter. "The Effects of Health and the Completed Fertility of Nonwhite and White U. S. Women Born Between 1867 and 1935." *Journal of Social History* 13 (1979): 191–217.

Degler, Carl. *At Odds: Women and the Family in America from the Revolution to the Present.* New York: Oxford University Press, 1980.

Easterlin, Richard. *The American Baby Boom in Historical Perspective.* New York: National Bureau of Economic Research, 1962.

———. "Factors in the Decline in Farm Family Fertility in the United States: Some Preliminary Research Results." *Journal of American History* 63 (1976): 600–614.

Englemann, George J. "The Increasing Sterility of American Women." *Journal of the American Medical Association* 37 (1901): 891–897.

Farley, Reynolds. *Growth of the Black Population: A Study of Demographic Trends.* Chicago: Markham Publishing Co., 1971.

Forster, Colin, and G. S. L. Tucker. *Economic Opportunity and White American Fertility Ratios, 1800–1860.* New Haven, Conn.: Yale University Press, 1972.

Gordon, Linda. *Woman's Body, Woman's Right: A Social History of Birth Control in America.* New York: Grossman, 1976.

Graff, Harvey J. *The Literacy Myth: Literacy and Social Structure in the Nineteenth-Century City.* New York· Academic Press, 1979.

Haines, Michael. *Fertility and Occupation: Population Patterns in Industrialization.* New York: Academic Press, 1979.

Hareven, Tamara K., and Maris A. Vinovskis. "Marital Fertility, Ethnicity, and Occupation in Urban Families: An Analysis of South Boston and the South End in 1880." *Journal of Social History* 9 (1975): 69–93.

Jones, Carl E. "A Genealogical Study of Population." *American Statistical Association Journal* 16 (1918–1919): 201–219.

Kantrow, Louise. "Philadelphia Gentry: Fertility and Family Limitation Among an American Aristocracy." *Population Studies* 34 (1980): 21–30.

Knowlton, Charles. *The Fruits of Philosophy, or the private companion of young married people*. New York, 1832.

Leet, Donald R. "The Determinants of the Fertility Transition in Antebellum Ohio." *Journal of Economic History* 36 (1976): 359–378.

———. "Human Fertility and Agricultural Opportunities in Ohio Counties: From Frontier to Maturity, 1810–1860." In *Essays in Nineteenth-Century Economic History: The Old Northwest,* edited by D. C. Klingaman and R. K. Vedder, pp. 138–158. Athens, Ohio: Ohio University Press, 1975.

Lindert, Peter H. *Fertility and Scarcity in America.* Princeton, N. J.: Princeton University Press, 1978.

McFalls, Joseph A., Jr. "The Impact of VD on the Fertility of the U. S. Black Population, 1880–1950." *Social Biology* 20 (1973): 2–19.

McFalls, Joseph A., Jr. and George S. Masnick. "Birth Control and the Fertility of the U. S. Black Population 1880–1980." *Journal of Family History* 6 (1981): 89–106.

Meeker, Edward. "Freedom, Economic Opportunity, and Fertility: Black Americans, 1860–1910." *Economic Inquiry* 15 (1977): 397–412.

Mohr, James C. *Abortion in America: The Origins and Evolution of National Policy*. New York: Oxford University Press, 1977.

Osterud, Nancy, and John Fulton. "Family Limitation and Age at Marriage: Fertility Decline in Sturbridge, Massachusetts, 1730–1850." *Population Studies* 30 (1976): 481–493.

Owen, Robert Dale. *Moral Physiology*. New York: Wright and Owen, 1831.

Reed, James. *From Private Vice to Public Virtue: The Birth Control Movement and American Society Since 1830*. New York: Basic Books, 1977.

Rosenwaike, Ira. *Population History of New York City*. Syracuse, N.Y.: Syracuse University Press, 1972.

Skolnick, M. et al. "Morman Demographic History. I. Nuptiality and Fertility of Once Married Couples." *Population Studies* 32 (1978): 5–19.

Vinovskis, Maris A. *Fertility in Massachusetts from the Revolution to the Civil War*. New York: Academic Press, 1981.

Wells, Robert V. "Family Size and Fertility Control in Eighteenth-Century America: A Study of Quaker Families." *Population Studies* 25 (1971), 73–82.

Wertz, Richard W., and Dorothy C. Wertz. *Lying-In: A History of Childbirth in America*. New York: The Free Press, 1977.

Yasuba, Yasukichi. *Birth Rates of the White Population in the United States, 1800–1860: An Economic Study*. Baltimore, Md.: John Hopkins University Press, 1962.

Chapter 3

Atwater, Edward C. "The Medical Profession in a New Society, Rochester, New York, 1811–1860." *Bulletin of the History of Medicine* 47 (1973): 221–235.

Bennett, Merrill K., and Rosamond H. Pierce. "Change in the American National Diet, 1879–1959." *Food Research Institute Studies* 2 (1961): 95–119.

Bonner, Thomas N. "The Social and Political Attitudes of Midwestern Physicians, 1840–1940: Chicago as a Case History." *Journal of the History of Medicine and Allied Sciences* 8 (1953): 133–164.

Cain, Louis P. "Raising and Watering a City: Ellis Sylvester Chesbrough and Chicago's First Sanitation System." *Technology and Culture* 13 (1972): 353–372.

Condran, Gretchen A., and Rose A. Cheney. "Mortality Trends in Philadelphia: Age- and Cause-Specific Death Rates 1870–1930." *Demography* 19 (1982): 97–123.

Curtin, Philip D. "Epidemiology and the Slave Trade." *Political Science Quarterly* 83 (1968): 190–216.

Deneven, William M., ed. *The Native Population of the Americas in 1492*. Madison, Wi.: University of Wisconsin Press, 1976.

Earle, Carville. "Environment, Disease, and Mortality in Early Virginia." In *The Chesapeake in the Seventeenth Century: Essays on Anglo-American Society & Politics,* edited by Thad W. Tate and David L. Ammerman, pp. 96–125. Chapel Hill, N.C.: University of North Carolina Press, 1979.

Fogel, Robert, and Stanley Engerman. *Time on the Cross: The Economics of American Negro Slavery*. Boston: Little Brown, 1974.

Gorer, Geoffrey. *The American People: A Study in National Character*. Rev. ed. New York: Norton, 1964.

Higgs, Robert. "Mortality in Rural America, 1870–1920: Estimates and Conjectures." *Explorations in Economic History* 10 (1972–1973): 177–195.

Jones, James H. *Bad Blood: The Tuskegee Syphilis Experiment*. New York: The Free Press, 1981.

Journal of Social History. Special issue on medical history. 10 (1977).

Kiple, Kenneth E., and Virginia H. Kiple. "Slave Child Mortality: Some Nutritional Answers to a Perennial Puzzle." *Journal of Social History* 10 (1977), 284–309.

Kubler-Ross, Elisabeth. *On Death and Dying*. New York: Macmillan, 1969.

Kupperman, Karen. "Apathy and Death in Early Jamestown." *Journal of American History* 66 (1979): 24–40.

Leavitt, Judith. *The Healthiest City: Milwaukee and the Politics of Health Reform*. Princeton, N.J.: Princeton University Press, 1982.

Leavitt, Judith, and Ronald Numbers, eds. *Sickness and Health in America: Readings in the History of Medicine and Public Health*. Madison, Wi.: University of Wisconsin Press, 1978.

McKinlay, John B., and Sonja M. McKinlay. "The Questionable Contribution of Medical Measures to the Decline of Mortality in the United States in the Twentieth Century." *Milbank Memorial Fund Quarterly* 55 (1977): 405–428.

Meeker, Edward. "The Social Rate of Return on Investment in Public Health, 1880–1910." *Journal of Economic History* 34 (1974): 392–419.

Mitford, Jessica. *The American Way of Death*. New York: Simon and Schuster, 1963.

Morgan, Edmund S. *American Slavery, American Freedom*. New York: Norton, 1975.

Rosenberg, Charles E. *The Cholera Years: The United States in 1832, 1849 and 1866*. Chicago: University of Chicago Press, 1962.

Rutman, Darrett B., and Anita Rutman. "Of Agues and Fevers: Malaria in the Early Chesapeake." *William and Mary Quarterly* 33 (1976): 31–60.

Shryock, Richard. H. *Medicine and Society in America 1660-1860*. New York: New York University Press, 1960.

Stannard, David E. *The Puritan Way of Death: A Study in Religion, Culture, and Social Change*. New York: Oxford University Press, 1977.

Stannard, David E., ed. *Death in America.* Special issue of the *American Quarterly.* 26 (1974).

Steckel, Richard H. "Slave Height Profiles from Coastwise Manifests." *Explorations in Economic History* 16 (1979): 363–380.

Vinovskis, Maris A. "Angels' Heads and Weeping Willows: Death in Early America." *American Antiquarian Society Proceedings* 86 (1976): 273–302.

Whorton, James C. *Before Silent Spring: Pesticides and Public Health in Pre-DDT America.* Princeton, N.J.: Princeton University Press, 1974.

———. *Crusaders for Fitness: A History of American Health Reform.* Princeton, N.J.: Princeton University Press, 1982.

Wood, Peter H. *Black Majority: Negroes in Colonial South Carolina from 1670 through the Stono Rebellion.* New York: Knopf, 1974.

Young, James H. *The Medical Messiahs: A Social History of Health Quackery in Twentieth-Century America.* Princeton, N.J.: Princeton University Press, 1967.

———. *The Toadstool Millionaires: A Social History of Patent Medicines in America before Federal Regulation.* Princeton, N.J.: Princeton University Press, 1961.

Chapter 4

Alger, Horatio, Jr. *Ragged Dick and Mark, The Match Boy.* New York: Collier, 1962.

Allen, David G. *In English Ways: The Movement of Societies and the Transferral of English Local Law and Custom to Massachusetts Bay in the Seventeenth Century.* Chapel Hill, N.C.: University of North Carolina Press, 1981.

Bernard, Richard M. *The Melting Pot and the Altar: Marital Assimilation in Early Twentieth-Century Wisconsin.* Minneapolis, Mn.: University of Minnesota Press, 1980.

Bowen, William A. *The Willamette Valley: Migration and Settlement on the Oregon Frontier.* Seattle, Wa.: University of Washington Press, 1978.

Buffon, Georges Louis Leclerc, Comte de. *Natural History, Geneal and Particular,* trans. by William Smellie, ed. 3, London: 1791.

Conzen, Michael P. "Local Migration Systems in Nineteenth-Century Iowa." *Georgraphical Review* 64 (1974): 339–361.

Cronon, William. *Changes in the Land: Indians, Colonists, and the Ecology of New England.* New York: Hill and Wang, 1983.

Daniels, George H. "Immigrant Vote in the 1860 Election: The Case of Iowa." *Mid-America* 44 (1962): 146–162.

Dreiser, Theodore. *Sister Carrie.* New York: Doubleday, 1900.

Faragher, John M. *Women and Men on the Overland Trail.* New Haven, Conn.: Yale University Press, 1979.

Farley, Reynolds. *Growth of the Black Population: A Study of Demographic Trends.* Chicago: Markham Publishing Co., 1971.

Fligstein, Neil. *Going North: Migration of Blacks and Whites from the South, 1900–1950.* New York: Academic Press, 1981.

Galenson, David W. *White Servitude in Colonial America: An Economic Analysis.* Cambridge, Eng.: Cambridge University Press, 1981.

Gastil, Raymond D. *Cultural Regions of United States.* Seattle, Wa.: University of Washington Press, 1975.

Gerlach, Russel L. *Immigrants in the Ozarks.* Columbia, Mo.: University of Missouri Press, 1976.

Goldthwaite, James W. "A Town that Has Gone Down Hill." *Georgraphical Review* 17 (1927): 527–552.

Grant, Madison. *The Passing of the Great Race or The Racial Basis of History.* New York, C. Scribner's Sons, 1916.

Handlin, Oscar. *Boston's Immigrants, 1790–1880: A Study in Acculturation,* rev. ed. New York: Atheneum, 1969.

———. *The Uprooted: The Epic Story of the Great Migrations that Made the American People,* 2nd ed. Boston: Little Brown, 1973.

Hareven, Tamara K. "Family Time and Industrial Time: Family and Work in a Planned Corporation Town, 1900–1924." *Journal of Urban History* 1 (1975): 365–389.

Higham, John. *Strangers in the Land: Patterns of American Nativism, 1860–1925.* New York: Atheneum, 1965.

Jeffrey, Julie R. *Frontier Women: The Trans-Mississippi West 1840–1880.* New York: Hill and Wang, 1979.

Jennings, Francis. *The Invasion of America: Indians, Colonialism, and the Cant of Conquest.* Chapel Hill, N.C.: University of North Carolina Press, 1975.

Johansen, Dorothy O. "A Working Hypothesis for the Study of Migrations." *Pacific Historical Review* 36 (1967): 1–12.

Johnson, Hildegard B. *Order Upon the Land: The U.S. Rectangular Land Survey and the Upper Mississippi Country.* New York: Oxford University Press, 1976.

Jones, Maldwyn A. *American Immigration.* Chicago: University of Chicago Press, 1960.

Jordan, Terry G. "Between the Forest and the Prairie." *Agricultural History* 38 (1964), 205–216.

Kiser, Clyde V. *Sea Island to City: A Study of St. Helena Islanders in Harlem and other Urban Centers.* New York: Columbia University Press, 1932.

Lee, Everett. "A Study of Migration." *Demography* 3 (1966): 47–57.

Menard, Russell R. "From Servant to Freeholder: Status Mobility and Property Accumulation in Seventeenth-Century Maryland." *William and Mary Quarterly* 30 (1973): 37–64.

Modell, John. "Tradition and Opportunity: The Japanese Immigrant in America." *Pacific Historical Review* 40 (1971): 163–182.

Orwell, George. *1984.* New York: Harcourt, Brace, 1949.

Powell, Sumner C. *Puritan Village: The Formation of a New England Town.* Middletown, Conn.: Wesleyan University Press, 1963.

Ravenstein, E. G. "The Laws of Migration." *Journal of the Royal Statistical Society* 48 (1885): 167–235; 52 (1889): 241–305.

Reps, John W. *Town Planning in Frontier America.* Princeton, N.J.: Princeton University Press, 1969.

Rolvaag, O. E. *Giants in the Earth.* New York: Harper and Brothers, 1927.

———. *Peder Victorious.* New York: Harper and Brothers, 1929.

Shepperson, Wilbur S. *Emigration and Disenchantment: Portraits of Englishmen Repatriated from the United States.* Norman, Ok.: University of Oklahoma Press, 1965.

Smith, Abbot E. *Colonists in Bondage: White Servitude and Convict Labor in America, 1607–1776.* Chapel Hill, N.C.: University of North Carolina Press, 1947.

Stein, Walter J. *California and the Dust Bowl Migration.* Westport, Conn.: Greenwood Press, 1973.

Steinbeck, John. *The Grapes of Wrath.* New York: The Viking Press, 1939.

Stilgoe, John R. *Common Landscapes of America, 1580 to 1845.* New Haven, Conn.: Yale University Press, 1982.

Taylor, Philip A. M. *The Distant Magnet: European Emigration to the United States of America.* New York: Harper and Row, 1971.

Thernstrom, Stephan. *The Other Bostonians: Poverty and Progress in the American Metropolis, 1880–1970.* Cambridge, Ma.: Harvard University Press, 1973.

Thernstrom, Stephan, ed. *Harvard Encyclopedia of American Ethnic Groups.* Cambridge, Ma.: Harvard University Press, 1980.

Thernstrom, Stephan, and Peter R. Knights. "Men in Motion: some Data and Speculations about Urban Population Mobility in Nineteenth-Century America." In *Anonymous Americans,* edited by T. K. Hareven, pp. 17–47. Englewood Cliffs, N.J.: Prentice-Hall, 1971.

Thomlinson, Ralph. *Population Dynamics: Causes and Consequences of World Demographic Change.* 2nd ed. New York: Random House, 1976.

Vogt, Evon Z., and Ethel M. Albert. *People of Rimrock: A Study of Values in Five Cultures.* New York: Atheneum, 1966.

Wacker, Peter O. *Land and People: A Cultural Geography of Preindustrial New Jersey Origins and Settlement Patterns.* New Brunswick, N.J.: Rutgers University Press, 1975.

Wade, Richard C. *The Urban Frontier: Pioneer Life in Early Pittsburgh, Cincinnati, Lexington, Louisville and St. Louis.* Chicago: University of Chicago Press, 1964.

Ward, David. *Cities and Immigrants: A Geography of Change in Nineteenth-Cenutry America.* New York: Oxford University Press, 1971.

Webb, Walter Prescot. *The Great Plains.* Boston: Ginn and Company, 1931.

Wells, Robert V. *Revolutions in Americans' Lives: A Demographic Perspective on the History of Americans, Their Families, and Their Society.* Westport, Conn.: Greenwood Press, 1982.

Wister, Owen. *The Virginian: A Horseman of the Plains.* New York: The Macmillan Co., 1902.

Wittke, Carl. *We Who Built America: The Saga of the Immigrant.* Englewood Cliffs, N.J.: Prentice-Hall, 1939.

Wright, Richard. *Native Son.* New York: Harper and Brothers, 1940.

Zelinsky, Wilbur. *The Cultural Geography of the United States.* Englewood Cliffs, N.J.: Prentice-Hall, 1972.

Chapter 5

Berkner, Lutz K. "The Stem Family and the Developmental Cycle of the Peasant Household: An Eighteenth-Century Austrian Example." *American Historical Review* 77 (1972): 398–418.

Byington, Margaret. *Homestead: The Households of a Mill Town.* Reprinted from 1910 edition. Pittsburgh, Pa.: University of Pittsburgh, 1974.

Carr, Lois G., and Lorena S. Walsh. "The Planter's Wife: The Experience of White Women in Seventeenth-Century Maryland." *William and Mary Quarterly* 34 (1977): 542–571.

Degler, Carl. *At Odds: Women and the Family in America from the Revolution to the Present.* New York: Oxford University Press, 1980.

Demos, John. *A Little Commonwealth: Family Life in Plymouth Colony.* New York: Oxford University Press, 1970.

Demos, John, and Sarane S. Boocock, eds. *Turning Points: Historical and Sociological Essays on the Family.* Chicago: University of Chicago Press, 1978.

Easterlin, Richard A. *Birth and Fortune: The Impact of Numbers on Personal Welfare.* New York: Basic Books, 1980.

Elder, Glen, Jr. *Children of the Great Depression: Social Change in Life Experience.* Chicago: University of Chicago Press, 1974.

———. "Scarcity and Prosperity in Postwar Childbearing: Explorations from a Life Course Perspective." *Journal of Family History* 6 (1981): 410–433.

Fischer, David H. *Growing Old in America.* New York: Oxford University Press, 1977.

Glick, Paul C. *American Families.* New York: John Wiley and Sons, 1957.

Glick, Paul C., and Robert Parke, Jr. "New Approaches in Studying the Life Cycle of the Family." *Demography* 2 (1965): 187–202.

Gordon, Michael, ed. *The American Family in Social-Historical Perspective,* 3rd ed. New York: St Martin's Press, 1983.

Greven, Philip J., Jr. *Four Generations: Population, Land, and Family in Colonial Andover, Massachusetts.* Ithaca, N.Y.: Cornell University Press, 1970.

Gross, Robert A. *The Minutemen and Their World.* New York: Hill and Wang, 1976.

Hareven, Tamara K., ed. *Family and Kin in Urban Communities, 1700–1930.* New York: New Viewpoints, 1977.

———. *Transitions: The Family and the Life Course in Historical Perspective.* New York: Academic Press, 1978.

Hareven, Tamara K., and Maris A. Vinovskis, eds. *Family and Population in Nineteenth-Century America.* Princeton, N.J.: Princeton University Press, 1978.

Laslett, Barbara. "Household Structures on an American Frontier: Los Angeles, California, in 1850." *American Journal of Sociology* 81 (1975): 109–128.

Laslett, Peter, ed. *Household and Family in Past Time.* Cambridge, Eng.: Cambridge University Press, 1972.

Modell, John, Frank F. Furstenberg, Jr., and Theodore Hershberg. "Social Change and Transitions to Adulthood in Historical Perspective." *Journal of Family History* 1 (1976): 7–32.

Rabb, T. K., and Robert I. Rotberg, eds. *The Family in History: Interdisciplinary Essays.* New York: Octagon Press, 1976.

Rutman, Darrett B., and Anita Rutman. " 'Now-Wives and Sons-in Law': Parental Death in a Seventeenth-Century Virginia County." In *The Chesapeake in the Seventeeth Century,* edited by Thad W. Tate and David L. Ammerman, pp. 153–182. Chapel Hill, N.C.: University of North Carolina Press, 1979.

Ryan, Mary P. *Cradle of the Middle Class: The Family in Oneida County, New York, 1790–1865.* New York: Cambridge University Press, 1981.

Stannard, David E. *The Puritan Way of Death: A Study of Religion, Culture, and Social Change.* New York: Oxford University Press, 1977.

Thornton, Arland, and Deborah Freedman. "The Changing American Family." *Population Bulletin* 38 (1983).

Uhlenberg, Peter R. "A Study of Cohort Life Cycles: Cohorts of Native Born Massachusetts Women, 1830–1920." *Population Studies* 23 (1969): 407–420.

Vinovskis, Maris A. "Angels' Heads and Weeping Willows: Death in Early America." *American Antiquarian Society Proceedings* 86 (1976), 273–302.

Walsh, Andrew S., and Robert V. Wells. "Population Dynamics in the Eighteenth-Century Mississippi River Valley: Acadians in Louisiana." *Journal of Social History* 11 (1978): 521–545.

Wells, Robert V. "Demographic Change and the Life Cycle of American Families." *Journal of Interdisciplinary History* 2 (1971): 273–282.

———. "Illegitimacy and Bridal Pregnancy in Colonial America." In *Bastardy and its Comparative History,* edited by Peter Laslett, Karla Oosterveen, and Richard M. Smith, pp. 349–361. Cambridge, Ma.: Harvard University Press, 1980.

Yans-McLaughlin, Virginia. "Patterns of Work and Family Organization: Buffalo's Italians." *Journal of Interdisciplinary History* 2 (1971): 299–314.

Index